WINDOWS 11

COMPLETE GUIDE

Taking You from Windows 11 Novice to Professional
In 33 Chapters

JAMES JODAN

Copyright © 2021 JAMES JODAN

All Rights Reserved

This book or parts thereof may not be reproduced in any form, stored in any retrieval system, or transmitted in any form by any means—electronic, mechanical, photocopy, recording, or otherwise—without prior written permission of the publisher, except as provided by United States of America copyright law and fair use.

Disclaimer and Terms of Use

The author and publisher of this book and the accompanying materials have used their best efforts in preparing this book. The author and publisher make no representation or warranties with respect to the accuracy, applicability, fitness, or completeness of the contents of this book. The information contained in this book is strictly for informational purposes. Therefore, if you wish to apply the ideas contained in this book, you are taking full responsibility for your actions.

Printed in the United States of America

CONTENTS

CHAPTER 1 1

GENERAL OVERVIEW OF WINDOWS 11 1

    WHAT IS WINDOWS 11? 1
    WHAT IS WINDOWS 11, AND WHY ARE YOU USING IT? 2
    WHAT'S NEW IN WINDOWS 11? 2
    WHAT IS MISSING FROM WINDOWS 11? 4
    WHY DOES WINDOWS 11 KEEP CHANGING? 5
    CAN MY CURRENT PC RUN WINDOWS 11? 6
    THE DIFFERENT EDITIONS OF WINDOWS 11 7

CHAPTER 2 10

GETTING STARTED WITH WINDOWS 11 10

    HOW TO INSTALL WINDOWS 11 INSIDER PREVIEW 11
    RECOMMENDED UPGRADE FOR WINDOWS 11 DEVICES 11
    OTHER WAYS TO INSTALL 11
    USING THE INSTALLATION ASSISTANT 11
    CREATING WINDOWS 11 INSTALLATION MEDIA 12
    WELCOME TO THE WORLD OF WINDOWS 12
    UNDERSTANDING THE USER ACCOUNTS 13
    KEEPING YOUR ACCOUNT PRIVATE AND SECURE 13
    SIGNING UP FOR A MICROSOFT ACCOUNT 14
    FIGURING OUT THE WINDOWS 11 START MENU 15
    LAUNCHING A START MENU PROGRAM OR APP 15
    FINDING STUFFS ON THE START MENU 15
    VIEWING, CLOSING, OR RETURNING TO OPEN APPS 15
    GETTING TO KNOW YOUR FREE APPS 16
    ADDING OR REMOVING START MENU ITEMS 16
    CUSTOMIZING THE START MENU 16
    HOW TO MOVE THE START MENU FROM THE CENTER TO THE LEFT SIDE 17

    ADDING FOLDERS IN THE START MENU 17
    HOW TO ORGANIZE THE PINNED APPLICATIONS 18
    EXITING FROM WINDOWS 19
    TEMPORARILY LEAVING YOUR COMPUTER 19
    LEAVING YOUR COMPUTER FOR THE DAY 19

CHAPTER 3 20

NAVIGATING WINDOWS' DESKTOP 20

    FINDING THE DESKTOP AND THE START MENU 21
    WORKING WITH THE DESKTOP 21
    LAUNCHING APPS WITH THE START MENU 21
    SETTING UP THE DESKTOP'S BACKGROUND 21
    RECYCLING INTO THE RECYCLE BIN 22
    MODIFYING UP THE TASKBAR 24
    SHRINKING WINDOWS TO THE TASKBAR AND RETRIEVING THEM 24
    SWITCHING TO DIFFERENT TASKS FROM THE TASKBAR'S JUMP LISTS 25
    CLICKING THE TASKBAR'S SENSITIVE AREAS 25
    SEEING THE ACTION CENTER AND NOTIFICATION 26
    VIEWING NOTIFICATION 26
    SEEING QUICK SETTING ICONS 26
    WATCHING WIDGETS 26
    CUSTOMIZING THE TASKBAR 26
    SETTING UP A VIRTUAL DESKTOP 27

CHAPTER 4 29

BASIC DESKTOP WINDOWS MECHANICS 29

    DISSECTING A TYPICAL DESKTOP WINDOW 29
    TUGGING ON A WINDOW'S TITLE BAR 29
    NAVIGATING FOLDERS WITH A WINDOWS ADDRESS BAR 30
    FIGURING OUT YOUR FOLDER NEW MENU BAR 30
    A QUICK SHORTCUT WITH THE NAVIGATION PANE 30

Moving inside a window with its scroll bar	30
Maneuvering windows around the desktop	31
Moving a window to the top of the pile Moving window to fill the whole desktop	32
Closing a window	32
Making a window bigger or smaller	32
Neatly placing windows side by side	32
Making windows open to the same darn size	32

CHAPTER 5 34

STORING AND ORGANIZING FILES 34

Browsing the file explore file cabinets	34
Getting the lowdown on folders	34
Peering into your drives, folders, and other media	34
Seeing the files on a drive	35
Seeing what's inside a folder	35
Creating a new folder	35
Renaming a file or folder	35
Selecting bunches of files or folders	36
Getting rid of a file or folder	36
Copying or moving files and folders	36
Seeing more information about files and folders	36
Writing to CDs and DVDs	37
Buying the right kind of blank DVDs and CDs for burning	37
Copying files to or from a CD or DVD	37
Working with flash drives and memory cards	37
One Drive: your cloud compartment	38
Setting up One Drive	38
Changing the One Drive setting	38
Opening and saving files from One Drive	39
Understanding which files live on One Drive, your PC or both	40

ACCESSING ONE DRIVE FROM THE INTERNET 40

CHAPTER 6 41

WORKING WITH PROGRAMS, APPS, AND FILES 41

STORING AN APP OR PROGRAM 41
OPENING A DOCUMENT 41
SENDING A DOCUMENT 42
CHOOSING WHICH PROGRAM SHOULD OPEN WHICH FILE 43
NAVIGATING THE MICROSOFT STORE 43
ADDING NEW APPS FROM THE MICROSOFT STORE APP 43
UNINSTALLING APPS 43
TAKING THE LAZY WITH A DESKTOP SHORTCUT 44
ESSENTIAL GUIDE TO CUTTING, COPYING, AND PASTING 44
SELECTING THINGS TO CUT OR COPY 45

CHAPTER 7 46

FINDING LOST FILES, APPS, OR PROGRAMS 46

FINDING LOST WINDOWS ON THE DESKTOP 46
FINDING CURRENTLY RUNNING APPS, PROGRAMS, AND GAMES 46
LOCATING A MISSING APP, PROGRAM SETTING, OR FILE 46
FINDING A MISSING FILE INSIDE A FOLDER 47
FINDING LOST PHOTOS 47
FINDING OTHER COMPUTERS ON A NETWORK 47

CHAPTER 8 48

PRINTING AND SCANNING YOUR WORK 48

PRINTING YOUR MASTERPIECE FROM THE DESKTOP 48
ADJUST YOUR WORK TO FIT ON THE PAGE 49
ADJUST THE PRINTER SETTINGS 50
CANCELING A PRINT JOB 51
PRINTING A WEBPAGE 51

TROUBLESHOOTING YOUR PRINTER 52
SCANNING FROM THE START MENU 53

CHAPTER 9 54

CRUISING THE WEB 54

WHAT IS AN ISP, AND WHY DO I NEED ONE? 54
CONNECTING WIRELESSLY TO THE INTERNET 54
BROWSING THE WEB WITH MICROSOFT EDGE 54
MOVING FROM ONE WEB PAGE TO ANOTHER 55
MAKING MICROSOFT EDGE OPEN TO YOUR FAVORITE SITE 55
REVISITING FAVORITE SITES 56
FINDING THINGS ON THE INTERNET 56

SAVING INFO FROM THE INTERNET 56
SAVING A WEBPAGE 56
SAVING TEXT 57
SAVING A PICTURE 57
DOWNLOADING A PROGRAM, MUSIC, OR ANY FILE 57

CHAPTER 10 58

NAVIGATING WINDOWS 11 PERIPHERALS: 58

MAIL, CALENDAR, AND TEAMS CHAT 58

ADDING YOUR ACCOUNTS TO WINDOWS 58
UNDERSTANDING THE MAIL APP SWITCHING AMONG THE MAIL APP'S VIEWS,
MENUS, AND ACCOUNTS 58
COMPOSING AND SENDING EMAIL 59
READING RECEIVED EMAIL 60
SENDING AND RECEIVING FILES THROUGH EMAIL 60
MANAGING YOUR CONTACTS IN THE PEOPLE'S APP 61
ADDING CONTACTS 61

DELETING OR REMOVING CONTACTS 62
MANAGING APPOINTMENTS IN CALENDAR MEETING ONLINE WITH TEAM CHAT
.... 63
STARTING TEAM CHAT 63
SENDING A TEXT MESSAGE 64
HOLDING VIDEO CHATS 64

CHAPTER 11 65

SAFE COMPUTING 65

UNDERSTANDING THOSE ANNOYING PERMISSION MESSAGES 65
STAYING SAFE WITH WINDOWS SECURITY.. 65
AVOIDING AND REMOVING VIRUSES 66
AVOIDING PHISHING SCAMS 67
SETTING UP CONTROLS FOR CHILDREN 67

CHAPTER 12 69

CUSTOMIZING SETTING IN WINDOWS 69

FINDING THE RIGHT SWITCH 69
ADJUSTING THE SYSTEM SETTINGS 69
CONNECTING AND CHANGING THE BLUETOOTH AND OTHER DEVICES. 70
CONNECTING TO NEARBY WI-FI NETWORKS AND THE INTERNET 71
PERSONALIZING YOUR PC LOOK AND FEEL... 72
FIXING AND REMOVING APPS 72
CREATING AND CHANGING ACCOUNTS FOR OTHERS 73
CHANGING DATE AND TIME AND LANGUAGE SETTING QUICKLY 73
SETTING UP FOR VIDEO GAMES 73
ADAPTING WINDOWS FOR YOUR SPECIAL PHYSICAL NEEDS......................... 74
MANAGING YOUR PRIVACY AND SECURITY 74
STAYING CURRENT AND SAFE WITH WINDOWS UPDATE............................ 74

CHAPTER 13 75

KEEPING WINDOWS FROM BREAKING **75**

BACK UP YOUR COMPUTER WITH FILE HISTORY 75
FINDING TECHNICAL INFORMATION ABOUT YOUR COMPUTER..................... 75
FREEING UP SPACE ON YOUR HARD DRIVE 76

CHAPTER 14 .... **77**

SHARING ONE COMPUTER WITH SEVERAL PEOPLE **77**

UNDERSTANDING USER ACCOUNTS 77
ADDING AN ACCOUNT FOR A FAMILY MEMBER OR FRIEND 77
CHANGING EXISTING ACCOUNTS 78
SEARCHING QUICKLY BETWEEN USERS 78
CHANGING A USER ACCOUNTS PICTURE 78
SETTING UP PASSWORD AND SECURITY 79
SIGNING IN WITH WINDOWS HELLO 79

CHAPTER 15 .... **80**

CONNECTING COMPUTERS WITH A NETWORK **80**

UNDERSTANDING A NETWORK PART 80
SETTING UP A SMALL NETWORK... 80
SETTING UP A WIRELESS ROUTER 80
SETTING UP WINDOWS COMPUTERS TO CONNECT TO A NETWORK 81
SHARING FILES WITH YOUR NETWORKED COMPUTER................................ 81
SETTING YOUR HOME NETWORK TO PRIVATE 81
SHARING FILES AND FOLDERS ON YOUR PRIVATE NETWORK........................ 81
ACCESSING WHAT OTHERS HAVE SHARED 82
SHARING A PRINTER ON THE NETWORK 82
SHARING WITH NEARBY SHARING... 82
TURNING ON NEARBY SHARING 82
SHARING FILES WITH NEARBY SHARING.. 83

CHAPTER 16 .... **84**

PLAYING AND COPYING MUSIC 84

    PLAYING MUSIC WITH THE GROOVE MUSIC APP 84
    HANDING MUSIC PLAYING CHORES TO WINDOWS 84
    STOCKING THE WINDOWS MEDIA LIBRARY 85
    BROWSING THE WINDOWS MEDIA LIBRARIES 85
    PLAYING MUSIC FILES IN THE PLAYLIST 85
    CONTROLLING YOUR NEW PLAYLIST ITEMS 85
    CREATING, SAVING, AND EDITING PLAYLISTS 86
    COPYING CDS INTO YOUR PC 87
    BURNING (CREATING) CDS 87

CHAPTER 17 88

FIDDLING WITH PHOTOS, VIDEOS, AND PHONES 88

    COPYING PHOTOS FROM PHONES AND CAMERA 88
    MAKING PHOTOS AND VIDEOS WITH WINDOWS CAMERA 88
    GRABBING PHOTOS FROM YOUR ANDROID PHONE WITH YOUR PHONE APP 88
    VIEWING COLLECTION OF YOUR PHOTOS 89
    VIEWING PHOTO ALBUM 89
    VIEWING SLIDESHOWS 89

CHAPTER 18 90

TROUBLESHOOTING YOUR WINDOWS 90

    RESETTING YOUR COMPUTER 90
    RESTORING BACKUPS WITH FILES HISTORY 90
    WINDOWS KEEP ASKING ME FOR PERMISSION 91
    RETRIEVING DELETED FILES 92
    I NEED TO FIX BROKEN APPS 92
    MY SETTINGS ARE MESSED UP 92
    I FORGOT MY PASSWORD 92
    FROZEN COMPUTER 93

CHAPTER 19 94

STRANGE MESSAGES ON YOUR PC 94

Add Microsoft account 94
Calendar notification 94
Choose what happens with this device................................... 94
Deleted files are removed everywhere 94
Did you mean to switch apps?... 94
Do you want to allow this app to make changes to your device? 95
Do you want to save changes?... 95
Enter network credential.. 95
How do you want to open these files? 95
Keep these display settings 95
Let's finish setting up 95
No usable drive Found.. 96
Save to one drive 96
Select to choose what happens with removable drives 96
Threat found... 96
USB device not recognized... 96
Verify your id on this pc 97
We are not allowed to find you 97
You do not have permission to access this folder 97
Your privacy setting blocked access to the location 97

CHAPTER 20 98

MOVING FROM OLD PC TO NEW WINDOWS 11 PC........................ 98

Moving to Windows 11, the Microsoft way 98
Having a third party to make the move 98
Buying lap links pc mover programs 98
Visiting a repair shop 98
Transferring files yourself 99

CHAPTER 21 100

HELP ON THE WINDOWS HELP SYSTEM 100

GETTING STARTED WITH WINDOWS 11... 100
CONTACTING SUPPORT 100

CHAPTER 22 101

TEN THINGS YOU WILL HATE ABOUT WINDOWS 11 AND HOW TO FIX THEM 101

KNOWING WHETHER YOUR PC CAN UPGRADE TO WINDOWS 11 101
THERE IS NO BACKUP PROGRAM 103
I WANT THE START BUTTON AND MENU IN THE LOWER-LEFT CORNER. 103
WINDOWS 11 KEEPS CHANGING 103
I DON'T WANT A MICROSOFT ACCOUNT 104
WINDOWS MAKES ME SIGN IN ALL THE TIME 104
I CAN'T LINE UP TWO WINDOWS ON THE SCREEN 104
IT WON'T LET ME DO SOMETHING UNLESS I'M AN ADMINISTRATOR 105
I DON'T KNOW WHAT VERSION OF WINDOWS I HAVE 105
MY PRINT SCREEN KEY DOES NOT WORK 105

CHAPTER 23 106

TIPS FOR TABLET AND LAPTOP OWNERS 106

USING THE NEW TOUCHSCREEN GESTURE 106
SWITCHING TO AIRPLANE MODE 106
CONNECTING TO A NEW WIRELESS INTERNET NETWORK......................... 106
TOGGLING YOUR TABLET SCREEN ROTATION 108
ADJUSTING TO A DIFFERENT LOCATION... 108
TURNING ON THE TRAFFIC WIDGET 108
ACCESSING THE MOBILITY CENTER... 108
BACKING UP YOUR LAPTOP BEFORE TRAVELING 109
TURNING CALCULATOR INTO A ROAD WARRIOR TOOL........................... 109

CHAPTER 24 110

DISK MANAGEMENT 110

How to manage disk and drive storage setting 110
Clean Up the Recommendation 111
Storage sense 111
Are you searching for storage detail? 112
Increasing decreasing the partition size of the drive 112
How to increase the size of the windows 11 partition 113

CHAPTER 25 114

WINDOWS KEYBOARDING 114

How to change your keyboard settings on windows 11 114
How to add a keyboard layout on windows 11 115
How to delete a keyboard layout on windows 11 115
How To Change Keyboard Layouts on Windows 11 116
How to activate the language input indicator on windows 11 117
Windows 11 New Keyboard Shortcuts 117
How to enable the touch screen keyboard on windows 11 118
How to enable the touch screen keyboard using the ease of access center 119
Clipboard 119
How to enable clipboard history on windows 11 120
How to use paste as plain text from clipboard history on windows 11 121

CHAPTER 26 123

WINDOWS FONT 123

Fonts 123
How to download and install fonts on windows 11 123
How to change your default font style on windows 11 124

PRIMARY MONITOR ON WINDOWS 11 127
  HOW TO CHANGE THE PRIMARY MONITOR OF YOUR COMPUTER 127

CHAPTER 27 128

WINDOWS 11 AS A VIRTUAL MACHINE 128

  WHAT IS A VIRTUAL MACHINE? 128
  ADVANTAGES OF VIRTUAL MACHINES 128
  HOW DOES A VIRTUAL MACHINE WORK? 129
  HOW TO CREATE A VIRTUAL MACHINE ON WINDOWS 11 129
  HOW TO INSTALL WINDOWS 11 TO A VIRTUAL MACHINE 133
  HOW TO INSTALL WINDOWS 11 ON RASPBERRY PI 4 135

CHAPTER 28 138

WINDOWS 11 PRODUCT KEY 138

  MEANING OF A PRODUCT KEY 138
  FINDING A WINDOWS 11 PRODUCT KEY 138
  HOW TO LOCATE A PRODUCT KEY USING THE COMMAND PROMPT 140
  BIOS 141
  HOW TO ENTER BIOS IN WINDOWS 11 141
  WHAT IS THE BEST WAY TO GET INTO BIOS FROM WINDOWS? 141
  USING THE FUNCTION KEYS 142
  USING THE WINDOWS SETTINGS APP 142
  ADVANCED STARTUP 144
  IP ADDRESS 146
  HOW TO FIND YOUR IP ADDRESS ON WINDOWS 11 146
  USING THE TASKBAR 146
  USING COMMAND PROMPT 147

CHAPTER 29 148

BLUETOOTH 148

  HOW TO ENABLE BLUETOOTH ON WINDOWS 11 148

How to repair Bluetooth using the windows troubleshooter 149
How to repair Bluetooth using the device manager...................... 150
How to screenshot on windows 11 151

CHAPTER 30.. 153

CORTANA 153

How to enable Cortana on windows 11 153
Command prompt 155
How to open command prompt on windows 11........................... 155
How to open command prompt using windows terminal 156
How to set command prompt as a default profile on windows terminal.. 156
Open Command Prompt from the Taskbar 157

CHAPTER 31.. 158

ANDROID APPS ON WINDOWS 11... 158

Applications 158
How to install android applications on windows 11 158

CHAPTER 32.. 163

CENTRAL PROCESSING UNIT (CPU).. 163

How to boost your processor or CPU speed on windows 11 163
How To Backup Your Files on Windows 11 166
How to create a full backup of your computer to an external hard drive on windows 11... 167
How to factory reset on windows 11... 170

CHAPTER 33.. 172

WINDOWS 11 SHORTCUTS KEYS 172

Newly Added Shortcuts in Windows 11 172
Text-Editing Shortcuts 173

GENERAL SHORTCUTS KEYS IN WINDOWS 11	173
FUNCTION SHORTCUT KEYS	177
FILE EXPLORER SHORTCUT KEYS	177
TASKBAR SHORTCUT KEYS	179
SETTINGS SHORTCUT KEYS	180
VIRTUAL DESKTOPS SHORTCUT KEYS	180
DIALOG BOX SHORTCUTS KEYS	181
COMMAND PROMPT SHORTCUT KEYS	182
GAME BAR SHORTCUT KEYS	183
ACCESSIBILITY SHORTCUT KEYS	184
BROWSER SHORTCUT KEYS	185

CHAPTER 1
GENERAL OVERVIEW OF WINDOWS 11

What Is Windows 11?

Windows eleven is the latest update of the Windows NT series. It is an upgrade from Windows ten and has come in at the right time, given the user's tendencies to get bored quickly. Since the inception of the windows series, it has been a norm for the windows company to upgrade their operating systems to optimize the user experience. Windows 11 is available as a free upgrade for any eligible windows ten user through the windows update.

According to Microsoft, this new upgrade promises a lot of new features and optimized performance. Most notably, in windows 11, there will be changes in the windows **shell,** and the **start menu** is completely redesigned.

From the first look of Windows 11, it does not look like the software you once knew, as even the **live tiles** have been replaced with a distinct **widget** panel where the taskbar is. With this feature, you can create sets of windows in compartments that can be minimized and grouped in the taskbar. Furthermore, with this upgrade, Microsoft teams are integrated into the windows shell.

There have been mixed reactions concerning the release of Windows 11. Its quality design is one of the reasons users love it. However, a look also gives the impression of regression with users needing to figure out how to use windows 11 again as they are not entirely user-friendly.

What is Windows 11, and why are you using it?

This is the big question for most laptops' users. Why do you have to use the windows software? Let's just say that a captain needs their ship. This analogy, as weird as it sounds, summarizes what Windows does on your laptop. Every human action done on your laptop has to be done with an operating system. Without Windows 11, you might as well buy a container instead of a laptop. Furthermore, your laptop at the startup screen will just say NON-system disk or disk error or insert system disk and press any key when ready. If you do not want any of these error messages, it is better to just install an operating system.

What's new in windows 11?

Every time windows come with a new operating system; you should be sure that it comes with some benefits. In windows 11, the changes are more pronounced, and right from the pack alone and screenshots of it, it is pretty clear that windows have a new look. It will not be seen as it has always been seen. Here are some of the new features in Windows 11:

Revamp of UI

Like its predecessors, there is a total revamp of the user interface, which goes along with a fluent design guide. This user interface pronounces more seamless usage and flexibility. With the revamp of the UI, there are new features to increase productivity and provide updates to security and accessibility while addressing the laggings in windows 10.

Redesign of the Microsoft store

The redesign of the Microsoft store comes in handy and comes with some extra features for developers to harness and enhance their productivity.

Microsoft teams

This collaborative platform is now available on the taskbar

Updates

One of the biggest complaints about windows ten users was that update sizes were too large. With this upgrade, update files are smaller and take less time. There is a big upgrade in browsing and wake time from sleep mode, which takes less time.

Linux Subsystem

While not in the initial installation, this feature has been earmarked for later in 2022. This permits users to install new android apps into their systems. You will need an Amazon account and a Microsoft account. Your pc also has to have 8Gb of ram to work with the app; while you can, through the Microsoft store, you can obtain android apps on the Amazon app store.

System security

System security has been taken to new heights as windows 11 can only work with trusted platform module 2.0, an important tool against firmware and hacks. Furthermore, it is required with windows 11 t have virtualization-based security VBS, hypervisor-protected code integrity, and secure boot. All of these features contribute to a safer experience using windows 11

What is missing from windows 11?

Microsoft is constantly evolving. This means that with every new installation or upgrade comes a new feature and some others dropped either for aesthetics or for the general functionality of your laptop.

Taskbar movement

Unlike in the other installation, the ability to move the taskbar will not be available to the Windows 11 users. This has come as a shock to many users as it means that most windows laptops might now be looking to uniform.

Combining open apps

Users will no longer have the ability to combine open applications

Dropping files into their icons in the taskbar

In the past, this feature used to be useful to users who wanted their work done easily and fast. With the new installation, you no longer have the chance to drag a file and drop them on their icons in the taskbar.

No events in Calendar Flyout

With the previous installation in windows 10, it was possible that your event would be displayed below the calendar where there is a fly-out. In the new installation, users have no recourse to this when they need to be reminded of events.

Features are missing in the Start Menu

There are no live tiles in a revamped windows 11 start menu. Furthermore, the start menu is non-resizable. So, with this feature left out, the new Windows 11 looks significantly different from what you know.

Why does Windows 11 keep changing?

The creators of windows have the responsibility of both keeping their users safe and promoting their experience. With this in mind, they must constantly bring new features that promote these as, without that, users might either get bored of the interface at the very least and the worst, all of their data is going to be susceptible to data breaches and hacks. So, simply windows 11 is a welcome development that promotes users' safety and experience.

Can my current PC run Windows 11?

The operating system that is allowed to run windows 11 is specific. You need at least a 7th generation intel core or AMD plus the second generation ryzen processor and a 4gig ram with at least 64 gig storage space, TPM 2.0, and finally, it has to support secure boot.

Looking at this requirement, we want to understand that it is strict. Nevertheless, the only reason it is so is to maximize the user's safety, and it is only computers that already have these features that can enjoy all of the benefits of windows 11. It is basically like a ps5 without a 4k television. You might still play it without the 4k television. But the only way your experience will be different from the ps4 experience is when you use a 4k tv.

Microsoft understands that it is essential to maintain reliability over a period, which usually implies **OEM and IHV** driver support. With these drivers, it is easier for Microsoft to manage the windows update in a coordinated fashion. And there is a better system that checks the device's health. With this, the reliability of the system with windows 11 is improved upon.

A trusted and **secure boot** is one requirement that is important to download windows 11. For systems integrated with safety boots that need both **UEFI** and **TPM, hardware** damage is minimal when the system is compromised. These two requirements ensure that hackers cannot gain access to your **bootkits** and **rootkits** and edit them.

Also, the requirements are so strict due to the high demands of windows 11 to run on devices. Systems that are not supported by windows 11 are 52% more susceptible to kernel crashes. And this is the most critical information to the user as they will have more peace of mind not installing windows 11 with unsupported devices. In contrast, supported devices are only likely to crash 0.2% of the time.

Finally, performance will be a problem with older devices trying to run windows 11; according to some tests run by Microsoft on older hardware, older hardware is simply not compatible and can become disastrous to your device health and even your overall user experience with windows.

The Different Editions of Windows 11

Windows 11 comes in seven different versions. They are windows 11 home; windows 11 pro; windows 11 pro-education; widows 11 pros for workstation; windows 11 enterprise; windows 11 education; windows 11 mixed reality.

So far, the only information we have about these different versions of windows is that the windows 11 pro has more features than the rest. However, in setting up your windows Home, you are going to need a Microsoft account.

Ultimately, the differences between the versions are going to be subtle, and the differences are going to be highlighted by who it is marketed for.

Based on Windows 10 editions, we can expect the new Windows 11 may have the 7 editions listed above. Different editions have different features and intended devices. You can check the introduction of the possible 7 Windows 11 editions below:

- **Windows 11 Home:** Most people will be using Windows 11 Home or Pro edition. The Home edition is designed for PCs and includes all features.
- **Windows 11 Pro:** As a popular Windows 11 edition, the Pro edition has all features of Windows 11 Home, but with some additional functions. The additional functions are designed for professionals and business environments.
- **Windows 11 Education:** Like Windows 10, Windows 11 Education will be also distributed through Academic Volume Licensing. It has fewer features than Windows 11 Home and Pro.
- **Windows 11 Enterprise:** The Windows 11 Enterprise edition has all features of Windows 11 Pro but with some extra features specially designed for IT-based organizations.

- **Windows 11 Pro Education:** This edition of Windows 11 contains most features of Windows 11 Pro. But it will come with some options disabled by default and it may add some extra options for usage in an education environment.
- **Windows 11 Pro for Workstations:** This edition of Windows 11 will be suitable for high-end hardware and is good for handling intensive computing tasks.
- **Windows 11 Mixed Reality:** A new edition of Windows 11 has been added. This edition is designed for mixed reality or virtual reality devices like Microsoft Hololens.

CHAPTER 2
GETTING STARTED WITH WINDOWS 11

This is where the biggest change comes in the new update of windows. This is one of the most important features of the windows as it acts as a master control panel for your search and where important applications and features can be found. While it is not the most advanced feature of the whole windows, it is still functional and works quite well, and is handy.

The first thing you might notice first is where the start menu is. Unlike in others, the start menu here is at the center of the screen. For many reasons, this has not gone down well with most windows users, and most are already finding devices on how to customize and move them to positions where we are used to them being.

While the start menu's position might be questionable, the argument for it being there in the center is that it improves navigation and adds some necessary improvement.

Furthermore, the start menu has a search bar that eases the ability of the users to search for a needed file or information online.

You also are going to have the ability to pin apps to the start menu

How to install windows 11 insider preview

You must know that windows 11 is not supported for all devices, and installing them into your device when it is unsupported can turn out to be disastrous to the life span of your device.

So having got that out of the way, we assume that your system is a supported device and can run windows 11 without crashing.

Recommended upgrade for windows 11 devices

If you are using windows ten and upgrading to Windows 11, it is just important to wait for the prompt notifying you that you can upgrade your device to check whether your device is ready for an upgrade,

To check for updates:

- Open the **start menu**
- Go to **setting**
- Go to **Update and Security**
- In windows update, you can check for an update

Other ways to install

Using the installation assistant

We do not recommend this for you unless you have been permitted to use this mode by support. After being instructed by support, you can go to the windows 11 download page to download the software.

Creating Windows 11 installation media

When you get to the windows 11 software download page, select create tool now and follow the instructions given to you to install windows 11.
There are two ways to install:
- You can upgrade your windows ten by launching the setup. There you can do a **full upgrade**—keeping personal file and windows settings as the default setting. Or you can do a **keep data only** upgrade, which keeps all of your files without the apps or the windows setting. And finally, a clean install that does not carry anything from the windows 11
- You can boot from the media and launch the setup. With this mode, nothing will be retained from your previous files or settings.

Welcome to the world of windows

When the setup screen appears, you will be instructed to designate the country or region you are from to input your preferred layout or method. Pick your preferred one and click yes.

With the next screen, after you click **next**, you can add another layout and language. If you don't want to need another, then you can just go ahead and click **next**.

With the next window comes the ability for you to review the windows license agreement after windows have successfully checked for any updates. You click **accept.**

The next page gives you the window to **name** your pc. Naming the pc is entirely your choice. You have to keep in mind that remembering the name can be good if you intend to use it on more than one pc. However, if you are using it isolated, it might be okay for you to use a generic name.

Understanding the user accounts

There are a lot of user accounts at your disposal. Depending on what you want to use it for and on what and whose system it is being installed in determines where the windows will be installed in. pick **set up for personal use** if you are installing it into your pc. Then you can use it later with a Microsoft or local account. Also, if the intention is for work or school, you might choose the **setup for work or school.**

Keeping your account private and secure

You must keep your account to yourself safe and secure. As you might have noticed by now, one of the greatest features of Windows 11 is its security. While windows do their part, you also have to do your part.

Signing up for a Microsoft account

You are going to need a Microsoft account to use windows 11. If you do not already have a Microsoft account, then this is the time that you should create one.

To sign up with your Microsoft account, enter your Microsoft account password and email address. If you have yet to have a Microsoft account, then you can **create one**.

The next interface prompts you to **create a pin** that will serve as an alternative to the Microsoft account.

When you click **to create** a **pin,** then you can use letters and symbols. Type the pin in and retype it in the box beneath and then click **okay.**

The next window notifies you if Windows recognizes the account logged in from another device and prompts you to **restore from Pc.** or **set up a new device.** Click **next** once you have checked your preferred setting.

Restoring from pc means that you copy settings and files from the previous device while setting up a new device lets you keep the system unique.

Read the privacy setting that comes next to make sure that you consent to their services.

Figuring out the windows 11 start menu

This is where the differences between Windows 11 and 10 become extraordinary. With the new Windows 11, the start menu's entirely new in appearance. There is s a search box at the top of the start menu, and there are icons that can be rearranged by dragging and dropping the icons from one place to the other. There is a new **recommended** section that shows apps and files that you have opened recently.

Launching a start menu program or app

Launching an app from the start menu is just as simple as clicking on the application you want to open, and immediately the application will be launched. If you need to confirm the prompt after clicking on the application, you might just read the prompt to access whether you can consent to it.

Finding stuffs on the start menu

You can find anything on your windows using the search box. comes in handy and can be helpful to help you find files, applications, and content both online and in your local drive

Viewing, closing, or returning to open apps

A welcome feature in windows 10 is also available on the windows 11 software as it allows the user to restore applications after you have shut down your pc. This can also be done with folders.

Getting to know your free apps

There are a lot of applications available to you on windows 11. They include power automated desktop, paint 3d, mail application. Etc. all of these applications make your windows functional, and you can work with them. to check all your apps, open the start menu and click **all apps** on the top right corner of the start menu

Adding or removing start menu items

To remove **start menu** items, simply open the **start menu** with the windows button and remove the item you want to remove by first right-clicking on it and then clicking **remove the item.**

Customizing the start menu

Windows eleven brings something new to the table, and you should be clear on that already by now. What makes this edition of windows better is that the user can edit every part of it. At the end of this part of the article, we hope that you will be able to customize your windows 11 start menu.

How to move the start menu from the center to the left side

The first thing you will observe with windows 11 is that the start menu is on the center of the screen instead of the left side. You can live it that way. But, for people like us who prefer things to traditionally stay the same, we expect that it should be left on the left side of the screen. Here is how to move it to the left side of the screen.
- Open your **windows setting.**
- Find the **personalization and go to the taskbar.**
- Find **taskbar alignment** where the **taskbar behavior** is
- Pick the **left** side in the drop-down that follows

Adding folders in the start menu

Like Windows ten, you are equally given the opportunity in Windows 11 to keep folders in the **start menu.** The process is pretty easy. Simply:
- Find the **setting**
- Go to the **personalization** menu
- Find the start page and select **folders**
  Once you follow the steps that we have just mentioned, then you can add any folder you wish to add to the start menu.
  Al of your folders immediately finds their way to the left side of the power menu, where the start menu is. From the start menu, you can access all of your important

documents without going through the long process of opening different applications.

However, to add a custom folder:
- Find the folder and right-click it
- In the interface that pops up, click **the pin to start** option.
- When you do this, the folder you have customized in the start menu will appear in the **pinned apps** segment of the start menu. This way you have a better-organized pc

How to organize the pinned applications

Pin apps to the Windows 11 start menu card. Rearrange the icons

It is significantly easier to have all of your important applications directly on the windows menu. So, most people tend to keep the applications therein earlier editions of Windows 11. So, maybe you want to learn how to attach all of your important applications to the start menu. Here is how:
- Select **all apps** where it is at the top right corner of your screen
- In the applications that slide down, scroll through and find the application that you want to pin unto the start menu
- When you find the application, right-click it, then get the **pin to start.** This can be done virtually anywhere.

- Immediately you finish what we have described, then your folder will immediately be pinned to the start menu.

For whatever reason, it can be necessary to be able to manually arrange the applications. This is as simple as it is done in windows ten and pretty much every other window.

- **Drag the application** within the **pinned section** to arrange it
- A second page is usually added when you pin more than 18 apps in the start menu. Just scroll through the pages to move through each of the pages.

Exiting from windows

This is the easiest thing to do with all devices. However, since this is an entirely new operating system, it might be tricky to do. So here is what to do.

Temporarily leaving your computer

You do not have to shut down your computer if you are just leaving it for a few minutes, as you can simply wait for it to go to sleep. Also, you can go to the start **menu** and select the power button and click **sleep.**

Leaving your computer for the day

You can shut your computer directly from the desktop by opening the **start menu** and clicking the **power** button

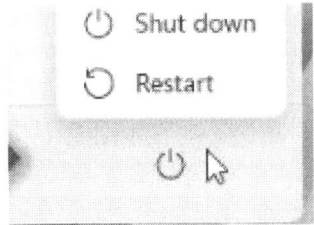

You can also shut down with the shortcut ALT+F4, which closes your app and gives you the option to either sign out, shutdown, research, restart, or switch users.

CHAPTER 3

NAVIGATING WINDOWS' DESKTOP

The desktop is where you will find the start menu. To improve flexibility and facilitate the user's ability to multitask, the new windows 11 is integrated with a new feature that will help you organize your windows with the new multi-desktop feature. Just, on the taskbar, select **task view** and pick **the new desktop.**

Now, you can open the app you intend to use on that desktop. However, you can switch between the desktops by picking the **task view.**

Finding the desktop and the start menu

The desktop is where your system launches into by default when you put it on your computer. It is generally empty until you open the **start menu.** Directly in the middle of the windows

Working with the desktop

The new Windows 11 comes with a new feature of adding multiple desktops. This means that Windows 11 has taken multitasking to a different level.

Launching apps with the start menu

You can launch apps directly from the Start menu by simply just opening the **start menu** either with the Windows key, then finding the app you want to open on the panel that pops by left/ double-clicking on it

Setting up the desktop's background

Just like in other windows versions, in Windows 11, you have the option to change and customize the background. It is just as simple as right-clicking on the desktop.

Then find **personalization**

When you click on personalization, **the background** comes next

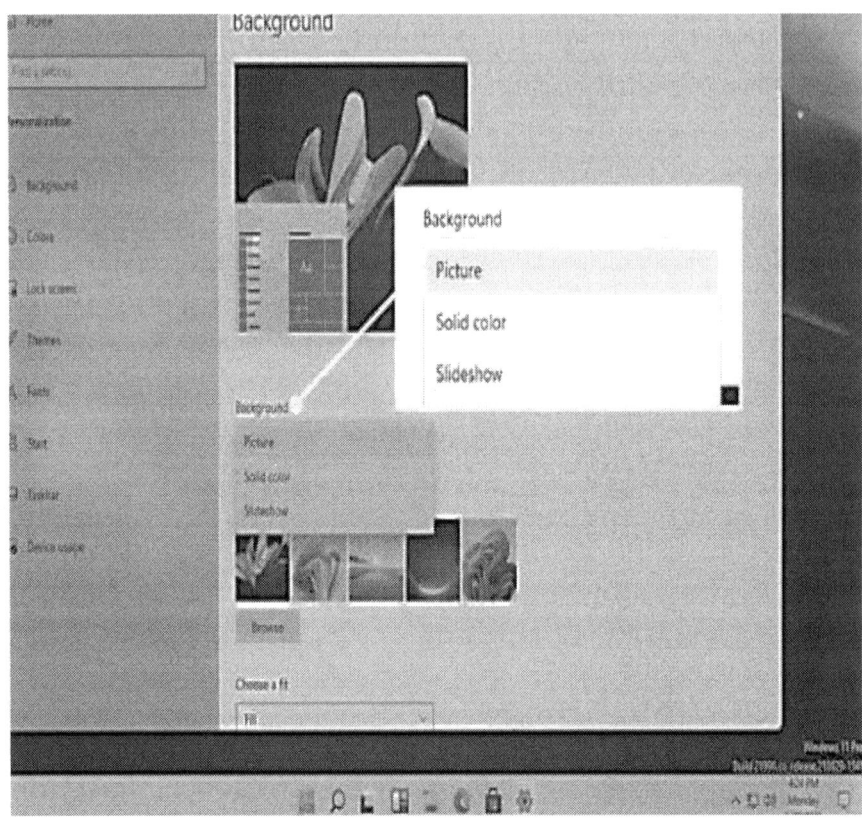

Choose how to customize your background by changing the **picture** or sprucing it up with **solid color** or a **slide show.** When you choose **a picture**, then you can browse through your local files to find the perfect picture for your system desktop

Recycling into the recycle bin

Whenever you are done with a file, simply place them in the recycle bin, and it will be stored there until you might need them again. However, if a period has passed, then they will be safely removed from the system. Nevertheless, you have the option to pick your preferred time that you want files in your recycle bin to be removed.

You can open the recycle bin in windows 11 by going to the desktop and clicking the recycle bin icon, which by default will be on the top left corner of your screen.

However, if you cannot find it there, then open the **settings** either from the start menu or by using the shortcut **Windows + I**

- Pick **personalization** on the left side of the setting panel, then click **themes** in the slide on the right side.
- Then open the **desktop icon set.**
- After doing this, check the **recycle bin** box and click **apply** and confirm with **okay.**

You can also find the recycle bin by searching for it on the windows start menu search box.

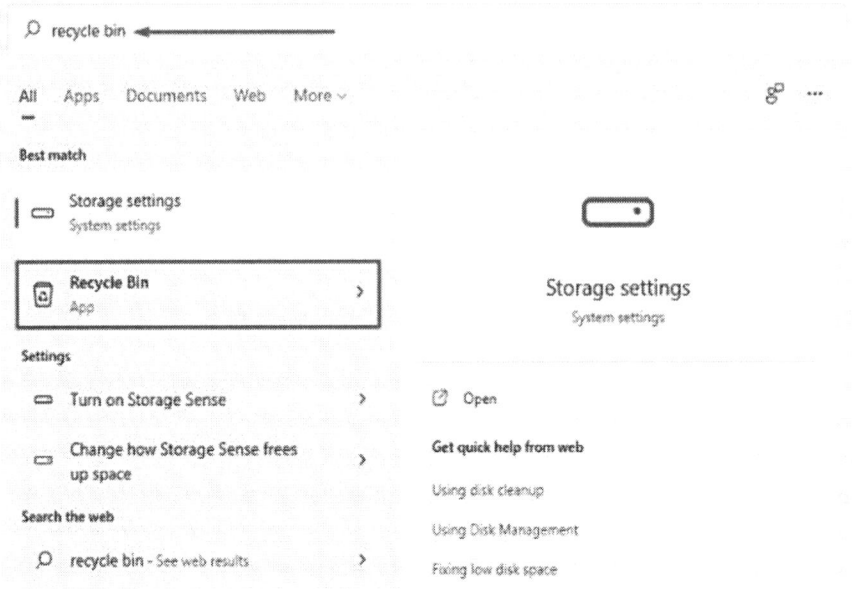

Modifying up the taskbar

The taskbar is one of the most important things on windows. However, if you have upgraded from windows 10 to 11, you will discover a few changes and somewhat downgrades. However, we can still provide you with ways to personalize and make your taskbar work for you as we wait for windows to add more features with the taskbar in subsequent upgrades

Shrinking windows to the taskbar and retrieving them

You can minimize open windows with the shortcut key by clicking on **windows + m.**

Also, you can maximize them by clicking **windows + shift + m**

Furthermore, if you only want to minimize the current window, you can do it with the shortcut **windows + down arrow**. To maximize that same app, while within the app, press the **windows + up arrow**

Switching to different tasks from the taskbar's jump lists

People who use windows ten are used to their jump list. All that needs to be done is just right-clicking on the application on the taskbar, and you will see everything you have been working on that app. However, in windows 11, it is quite different by default.

- So, go to **settings**
- on the search bar, click **start settings**

You will find the **jump list setting** there. All you have to do now is to toggle the one and off button to activate or deactivate the jump list.

Clicking the taskbar's sensitive areas

The taskbar is a sensitive area in your windows, and it is where a lot can be found. It makes work easier and gives you a notification when there is a need for it.

Seeing the action center and notification

This can be found on the right side of the taskbar and, at first glance, share similarities with Windows 10; however, they are ultimately different.

Viewing notification

Your notification is now going to pop where the date and time are. To check the notification interface, however, you need to click the date and time, which also makes the calendar pop up. It is above the Calendar that your notification can be managed.

Seeing quick setting icons

to do this, simply press the **windows + A** shortcut, and your quick setting is going to be opened up quickly. Furthermore, in the action center, you can turn on the Wi-Fi or enable some ease of access functions as well as toggling on the Bluetooth or night light.

Watching widgets

You can access your widgets either through the widget button paced on the taskbar or by clicking **Windows+ w.** here you will find the news, the weather update, etc.

Customizing the taskbar

there is only a lot you can do with the new Windows taskbar. However, you can still customize it. To do this, go to **settings,** then **personalization.** Find the **taskbar** and then go to the **taskbar behavior.** Here you have a lot of options to choose from to customize your taskbar.

You can remove applications pinned to the taskbar by right-clicking on the icon on the taskbar and clicking **unpin.**

Setting up a virtual desktop

Virtual desktops aren't new to Windows. In Windows 10, it was a simple matter to create a separate desktop so that, for example, you could have one desktop for one project and a second for another, or one for your work and a second for your other kinds of stuff.

However, in Windows 11, there has been an upgrade. Now, you can also have a different wallpaper for each desktop, making it easier to distinguish one from another (and offering you a different mood, depending on what you're using it for). And several other features make the use of virtual desktops easy and efficient. Note that some of these were introduced in Windows 10, but together with the new features of Windows 11, they make a handy toolbox.

To create a new virtual desktop:

- Hover over or click on the "Task view" icon in your taskbar (it's the one that looks like one square superimposed on another).
- Click on the "New desktop" thumbnail. Find the virtual desktop on your taskbar, then click on it

You can also use the key combination **Win + Ctrl + D;** in that case, you'll immediately find yourself on your new desktop.

You can now place different apps on your separate desktops. Move from one desktop to the other by clicking the "Task View" icon. (You can also move around by using the familiar **Alt-Tab** key combination, which will take you to all the apps on one desktop and then to the apps in the next.)

To remove a desktop:

- Hover over or click the "Task View" icon.
- Hover over the virtual desktop you want to remove and click the "X" in the upper right corner.

CHAPTER 4

BASIC DESKTOP WINDOWS MECHANICS

Dissecting a typical desktop window

A typical window does a task. So, when you open a window, it takes a part of the screen. You can open as many windows as possible on your desktop. However, for the organization, simply close your windows after you use it

Tugging on a window's title bar

Just like in Windows 10, you have the option to toggle on your windows title bar to make sure that all of the other apps are minimized without manually going to minimize the other open windows one by one. All you have to do is hold the title bar and shake it.

By default, the setting is deactivated. So, go to the **settings** then the **system.**

While in **the system,** click **multitasking.**

Then scroll down to find the option by your left to turn on the title bar windows shake.

Navigating folders with a windows address bar

Windows 11 also has an address bar that will be available to you to make sure that you can easily find documents on the file explorer.

Figuring out your folder new menu bar

Here you get a menu bar on file to explore to ensure that you have more options navigating and finding documents on file explorer.

A quick shortcut with the navigation pane

The quick shortcut on the navigation pane makes you enter an address to find a folder or file easily. As far as you remember, the directory.

Moving inside a window with its scroll bar

By default, when a scroll bar is not in use, then they are hidden. However, to keep them on, go to settings on the **start menu** and find **accessibility,** then open the **visual effects.** Then toggle between on and off to hide or show the scroll bar. They will be on the left side of the screen and allow you to navigate through the page that you are on.

Boring borders

- If you do not like how your borders look, you can simply go to **settings** from the start menu.

- Then find and open **personalization** on your right and open **colors** on the left.
- Here you will find all the available colors.
- toggle **on** to show the color you have picked in the border

Custom colors	View colors
Show accent color on Start and taskbar	Off
Show accent color on title bars and windows borders	On

elated settings

Maneuvering windows around the desktop

Like other versions of windows, you can move windows by carrying the title bar and carefully maneuvering them across the desktop to where you want it to be.

Moving a window to the top of the pile moving window to fill the whole desktop

To move a window to the top of the pile, simply click on it or the border, and it will stand out.

Closing a window

Windows 11 still has the close button on most apps, so clicking on it closes the app. Or you can force quit a window with the hotkey **alt+4**

Making a window bigger or smaller

you have the option to minimize windows by resizing them with your mouse. Simply go to the rim of the app and let the mouse turn into a hook. Then, resize it

Neatly placing windows side by side

to place windows side by side, just move the two windows you want to place side by side to the opposite side of the screen, and immediately windows automatically make them share half of the screen

Making windows open to the same darn size

Resize the windows to the size you want them to be, then close them, and immediately, the windows is going to remain the same as it memorizes the previous size it was when it was last used.

CHAPTER 5
STORING AND ORGANIZING FILES

Browsing the file explore file cabinets

Not everything has changed in windows 11. Some things are still the same. You can save your files in an open folder on the file explorer.

Getting the lowdown on folders

Folders are where all of your files are stored. To access it, simply click on it twice, and it is going to be opened. They often look as shown below:

Folders make all of your files organized. To create one, click **new** on the top left corner of the file explorer.

Peering into your drives, folders, and other media

When you open a drive, you see all of the files and media available in it. so, with

Seeing the files on a drive

Files on the drive include folders, media, etc., and important software. Writing on drives might require some extra permission as deleting folders on the drive might adversely affect installed software.

Seeing what's inside a folder

The same things inside folders are the same things inside drives. They include other folders, files, and media and can be named and renamed to be found easily.

Creating a new folder

To create a new folder, you can click on the **new** icon on the top left corner of the file explorer screen, and also, you can right-click on a space in a folder, and the option will pop up for you to add **a new folder**.

Renaming a file or folder

To rename a file or folder, right-click on it and find **rename.** You can also just left-click once on the icon and then rename it. However, you can also use the **CTRL+left/right** to move between cursor. You can also use **CTRL+delete/backspace** to delete the words.

Selecting bunches of files or folders

To select many files, you can do with the mouse by holding an empty part of the screen and dragging it over files that you want to select.

Or

You can hold **CTRL** and select any file you want to pick by clicking them while you hold **CTRL.**

Getting rid of a file or folder

To delete a folder, simply select it and right-click on it—you will find **delete.** Click on that

Copying or moving files and folders

to copy files, simply select them and right-click on them. then you can either click **copy** or **cut** and move them to the file that you want them to be in

Seeing more information about files and folders

to see more information about the files and folder, simply right-click and go to **Properties.** In **properties**, you are going to find more information about the folder. Also, selecting or hovering over the folders will provide you with information you need in the folder and file

Writing to CDs and DVDs

Burning into CDs and DVDs can be a way to copy and share files across devices. Windows 11 also permits you to write CDs and DVDs as far as it is the right kind.

Buying the right kind of blank DVDs and CDs for burning

there are two types of CDs to be bought. They are: CD-R and CDRW—the CDR is cheaper but cannot be rewritten once it is filled. However, you can rewrite on a CD-Rw. The same goes for DVDs. The r cannot be rewritten, while RW can be rewritten.

Copying files to or from a cd or DVD

To copy a file, simply select the file and drag them to your preferred directory. Furthermore, you can also right-click on the file and select **copy** or **cut.** Then **paste** it to your preferred directory. After copying or cutting a file, right-click on an open space in the directory you want to move the file into and **paste** it there.

Working with flash drives and memory cards

Windows 11 works with flash drives and memory cards. When attached, the name of the flash drive or memory card will be found there so you can access them like every other folder or drive on your computer

One drive: your cloud compartment

One drive is a modern innovation launched by Microsoft in August 2007, giving users the access to store all of their files and personal data and sync them across different devices.

You might have heard of it or have seen it on your computer—especially on modern computers. Microsoft one drive is an efficient tool that uses a cloud database system to store your entire document. Whether it is for your usage, office usage, or school, there are a lot of plans for you as an eligible client to store your entire helpful document. They are a convenient device and super effective and efficient at safely and securely handling all your documents and files from your computer. Anywhere you go, your files are just a click away from you.

Setting up one drive

To set up one drive

- Go to the **file explorer** and click the **one drive icon**
- Then select create an account if you don't have one already or sign in if you already have one after placing your Microsoft email.

Changing the one drive setting

To change settings;

- Go to the one drive on your taskbar and open it

- You will see the **settings** icon.
- Open It, and you will be able to personalize one drive

Opening and saving files from one drive

One drive works like every other folder on your computer. The only difference is that the files in one drive are synced online. So, if you want any files saved, put them in one drive.

Understanding which files live on one drive, your pc or both

You can save files on one drive and make them available on your laptop.

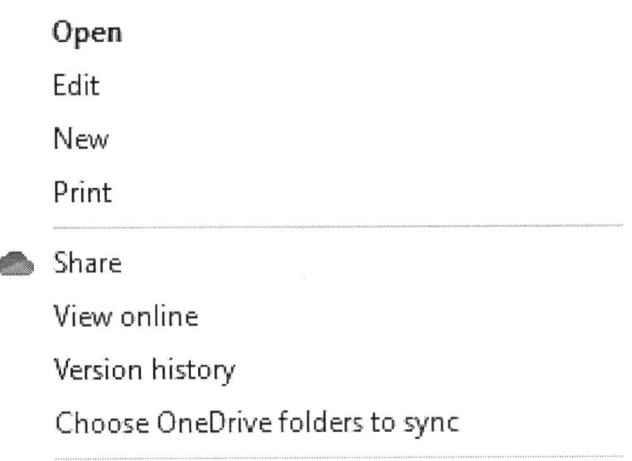

You can keep files saved on your pc and also backed online. Then you can delete them from your pc and make them only available offline. OneDrive is a cloud hard drive.

Accessing one drive from the internet

One drive can be accessed on the internet by going to onedrive.live.com. Here you will find all of your backed up and saved files.

CHAPTER 6
WORKING WITH PROGRAMS, APPS, AND FILES

To get to any of your apps, you can use the Windows 11 search tool to find any application that might be otherwise hard to find. Click the **start menu,** and on the top corner, you should see the search box. Type whatever keyword you are looking for, and some relevant suggestions of the application would pop up, Whether online or on your hard drive.

Generally, some applications can be pinned to the start menu, desktop or taskbar, so that they can be easily found. To pin apps to the taskbar, open the application and right-click on the running app in the toolbar. Then select **pin to taskbar.**

Storing an app or program

It is advisable to only buy or install applications from trusted sites as that reduces any chance of your system contracting a virus. The recommended platform for windows 11 is the Microsoft store which can be found pinned to the start menu.

Opening a document

Documents and relevant files are usually opened in the **file explore the** application. But you also have the option to search for them in the **start menu's search box.**

Sending a document

You can send documents to virtual drives or different directives in your system. Just:

- right-click on the document

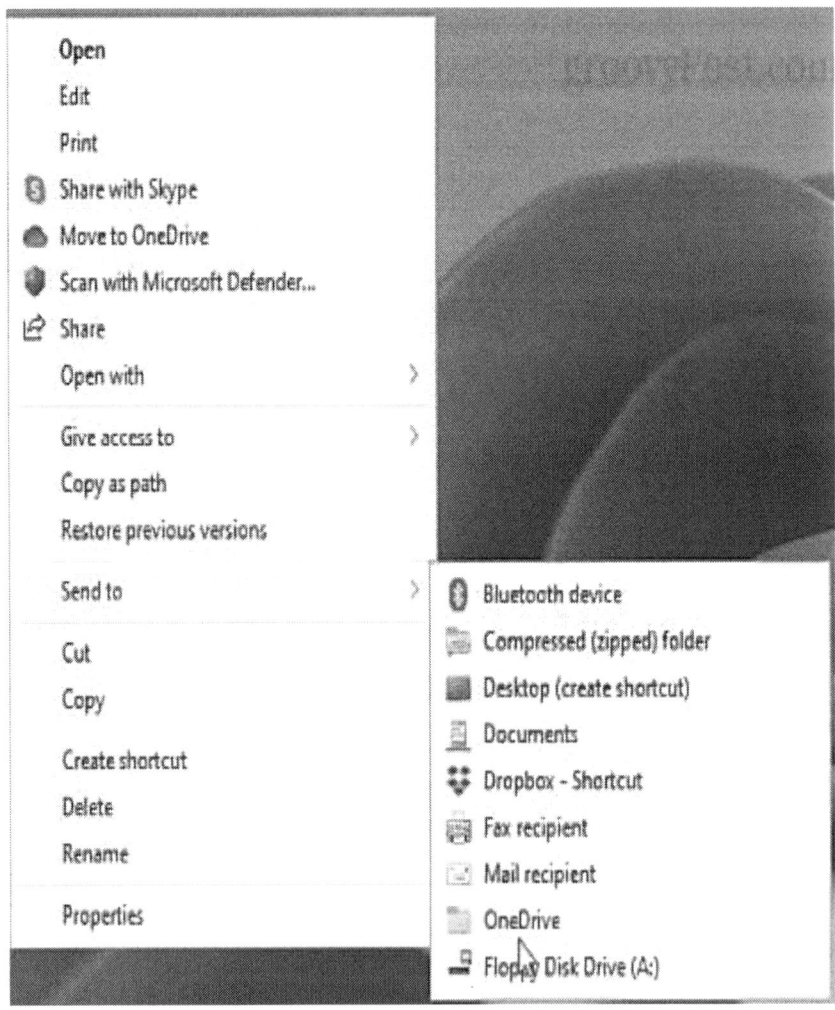

- find **send to** the inbox that appears and see where you want to send the copy to

Choosing which program should open which file

By default, your files will be opened by the recommended applications in your system. However, if you want to open with a different program or application, you can just find the file and right-click on it. then in the text box that comes next, select **open with**

Navigating the Microsoft store

Unless if you have removed it from there, your Microsoft store box would be found in your **taskbar. However,** you can also simply search for it in the **start menu' search box**.

Adding new apps from the Microsoft Store app

Click the **application** icon on the Microsoft store to have access to all the available, accessible, and paid apps.

Uninstalling apps

Maybe you are running out of space or just feel that you need to cut down the amount of application in your system. Windows 11 has provided a better way to do this. Simply:

- go to the **start menu**
- find **all apps** on the top left corner of the start menu

- when you have opened **all apps,** just right-click on the application, and a text box will provide the option to uninstall.

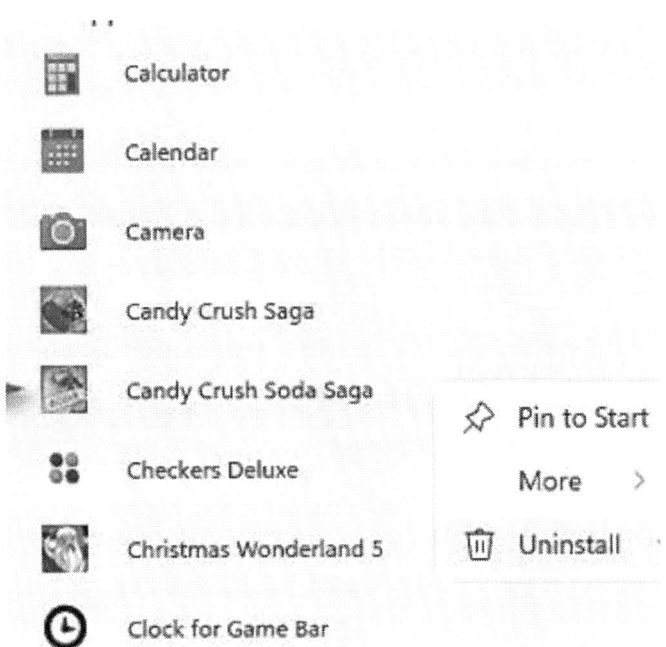

- Click **uninstall**, and you will no longer have access to that program or application.

Taking the lazy with a desktop shortcut

The **windows+D** shortcut still works in windows 11 hold the two keys together to jump to the desktop.

Essential guide to cutting, copying, and pasting

When you cut and paste, you are essentially moving a file from one directory to the other. However, when you copy and paste, you are making a duplicate copy of a file in a different or the same directory. To do this, select the file and use the shortcut **Ctrl C** to copy a file. But, use **ctrl x** to cut the file. Then go to the preferred directory to paste it with ctrl v. this feature works the same way it does in windows 11

The quick guide to copy, cut and paste

- Ctrl c-copy
- Ctrl x—cut
- Ctrl v--paste

Selecting things to cut or copy

you can select a file with your mouse by clicking on them once. However, if you want to select multiples, you can hold the mouse in an empty area of the screen and slide over files you want to select. You can also hold the **ctrl** button as you pick the files one by one.

CHAPTER 7

FINDING LOST FILES, APPS, OR PROGRAMS

Are you looking for an application or window? Well, let's help you find them.

Finding lost windows on the desktop

Your windows can not get lost on your system. The only problem will be how to find it. You can use the alt+tab key to see any window on your application. Just hold the two buttons together, and all the available open windows and apps will be available to you

Finding currently running apps, programs, and games

to find a running app, use the short key **alt+tab**, and you will find all the available app that is running on your system

Locating a missing app, program setting, or file

Unless you have deleted an app, they should be easy to find. You can use the start menu' search box to find a missing app, or you can go to **settings** with **set + I** and go to **apps>apps and features.** To find a complete list of all the available apps running on your Windows 11

Finding a missing file inside a folder

To find a missing file, you can use the search box on the start menu, or you can go to file explore> PC and use the search box to search for the file you are looking for thoroughly.

Finding lost photos

Most pictures are saved in **images** on your **file explorer**. Go to the file explorer, and on the left pane, you will see a list. In that list**, photos** would be written next to the icon. In that folder, you can find all of your relevant pictures

Finding other computers on a network

to see other users in your network, just go to the file explorer and click **network**. Here you will find all the computer that is connected to yours.

CHAPTER 8

PRINTING AND SCANNING YOUR WORK

This is one of the most important things to learn how to do with windows 11, as sometimes getting work into and out of paper can make a difference at work.

To print means that you want to convert a page on your desktop into paper. In contrast, to scan implies that you want to make a digital copy of a document.

So, let me show you how to do this

Printing your masterpiece from the desktop

The new Windows 11 offers you the option to print your work. There are a few options to choose from.

- You can select print from the program's file option.'
- Select the print icon
- You can right-click on a document and select print
- You can get a pic a document and drag them onto your program's toolbar
In the dialog box that usually appears next, select **OK** then all of the files will be immediately sent to your printer for printing

Adjust your work to fit on the page

Sometimes you need what you want to print to fit on the page. This is what the dialogue box that comes next is for. You can use it to make the intended print

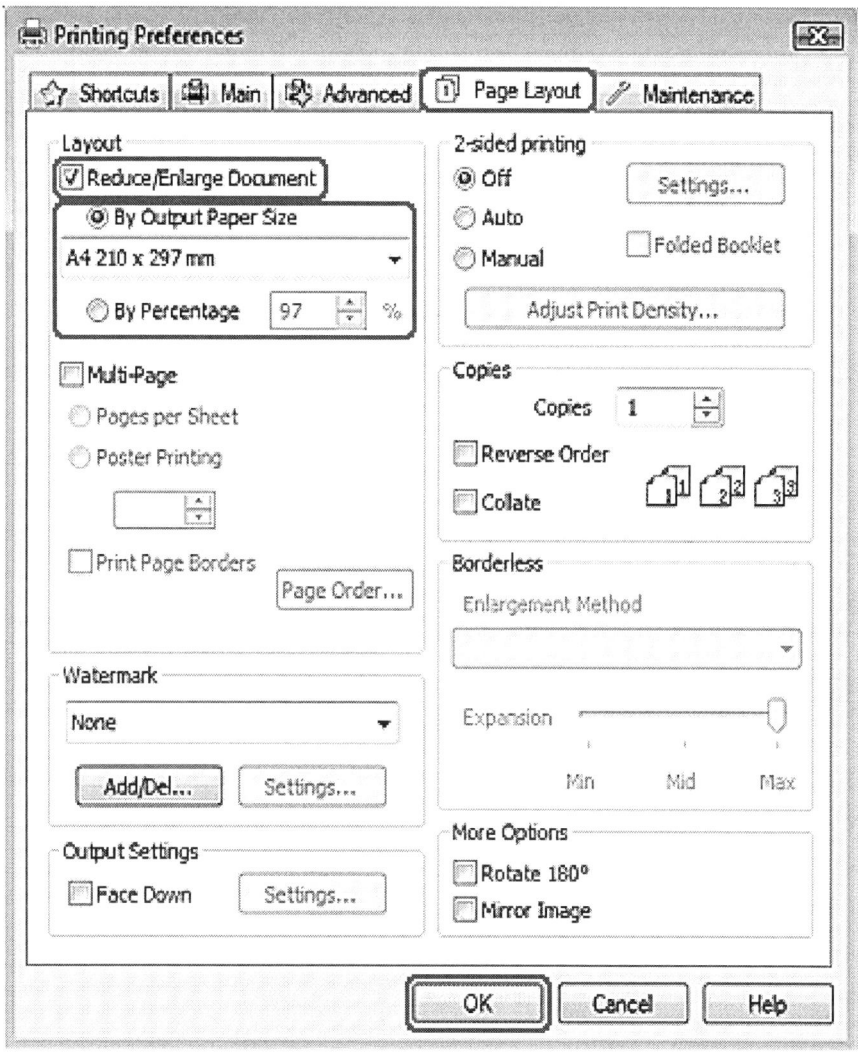

in the figure above, you should observe that you can edit how you want the job to be on your paper

Adjust the printer settings

To get to your printer setting, connect the printer, and in the dialogue box before printing (as shown below)

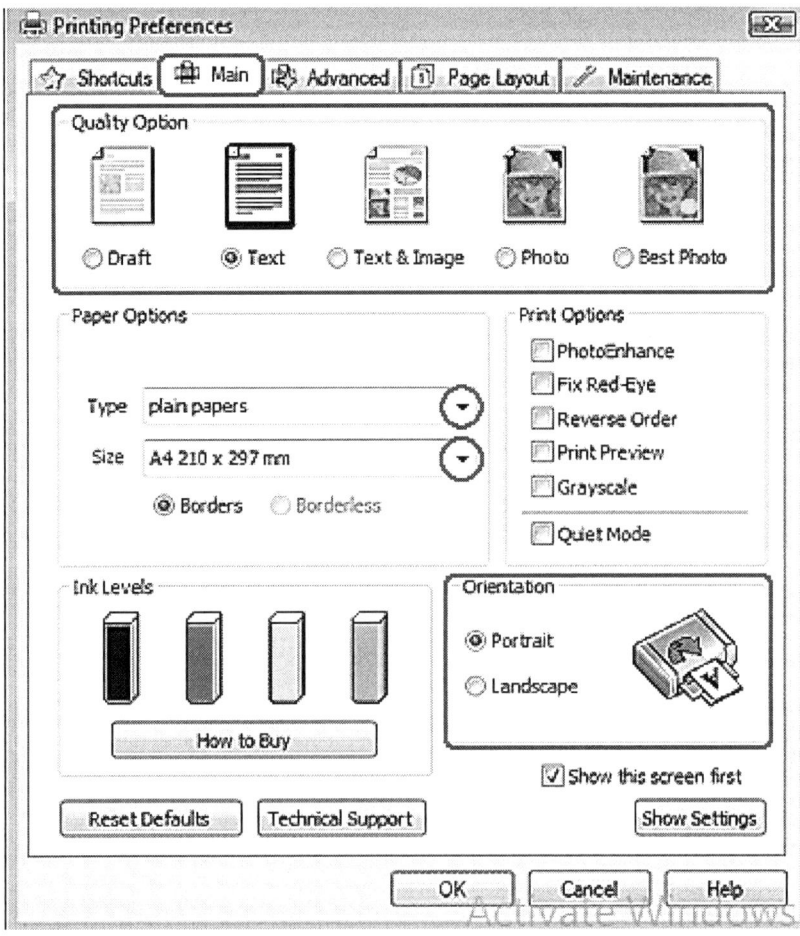

here, you can fix the appropriate setting and size. If you want your document orientation to be in landscape or portrait, you can fix that here. Also, you can fix the page layout. Once you are done with the setting, then click OK.

Canceling a print job

- Once you start a print job on your computer, you should see a printer icon on your action center; open it
- When a menu pops up, pick **open all active printers or printer queue**
- Then right-click on the print job that you intend to cancel and select Cancel.
- In the prompt that comes next, select **yes**

Printing a webpage

To print a webpage:

- Open the webpage in your browser
- Click the menu option on the left corner of the browser (e.g., chrome or Firefox) represented by three vertical dots.

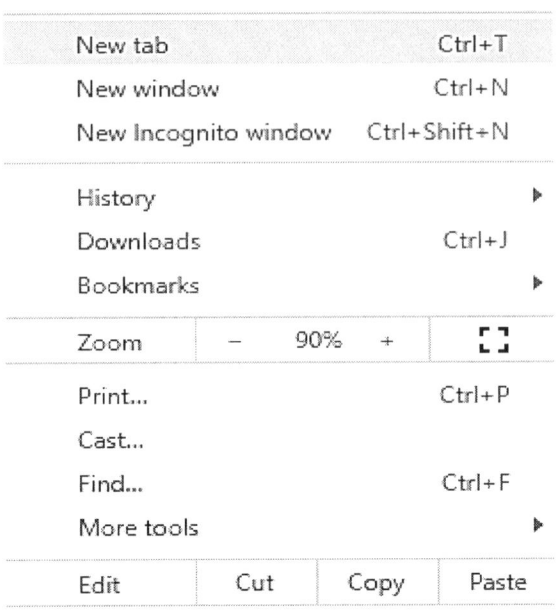

- Select **print** and follow the direction in the dialogue box that comes next

Troubleshooting your printer

To troubleshoot your printer, follow the step below

Go to **setting** and find **troubleshoot**

Go to **other troubleshooter**s in the **troubleshooter** interface and select **run** to troubleshoot

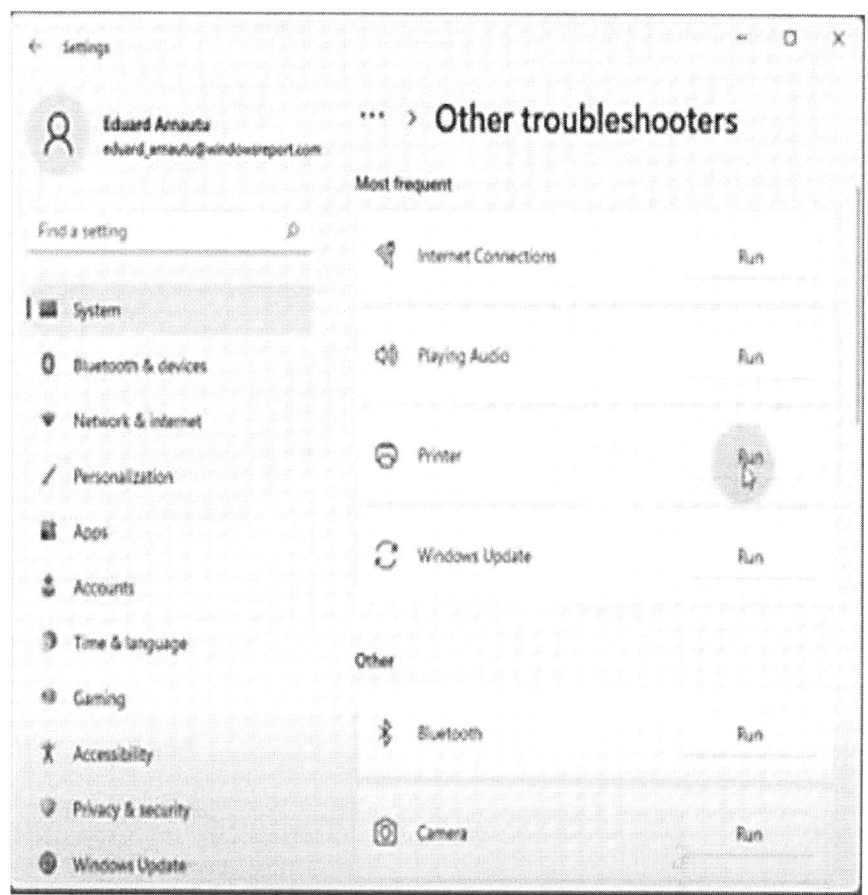

Scanning from the start menu

To scan a document, you need a scanner connected to your pc. Once connected, it will become available on your pc, and any document placed on the scanner can be processed on your desktop.

CHAPTER 9

CRUISING THE WEB

In the age of information that we live in, the web is increasingly important to us. It is where some work, some shop, and others interact with long-lost friends. this is a feature that never changes with every new information, and we would like to get you conversant with how to cruise the web.

What is an ISP, and why do I need one?

Simply ISP is the acronym for an internet service provider. Without it, you will not be able to have access to the internet. You will need an ISP to gain access to the internet.'

Connecting wirelessly to the internet

- Go to the **Quick setting** and click network or hold **window + A**
- select the arrow next to the wireless icon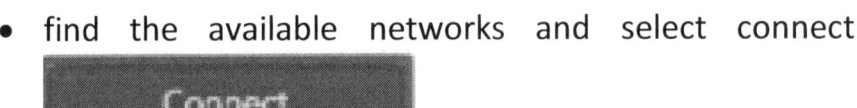
- find the available networks and select connect

Browsing the web with Microsoft edge

Microsoft Edge is the default browser for Microsoft operating system. You should find it pinned to the taskbar of your system. Just left-click or double-click to open it, and you are going to have access to a wide array of sites on the internet.

Moving from one web page to another

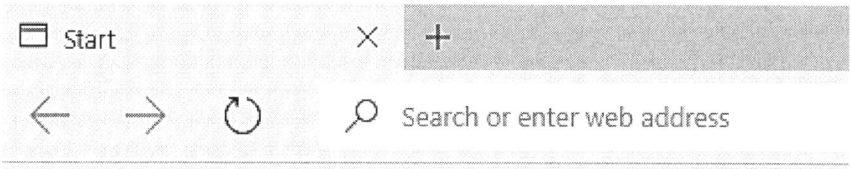

In Microsoft edge and in like every other browser, you can explore pages.

- Select the **back arrow** to go to the previous page
- Select the **forward arrow** to go to the next page
- And if you want to create a new page, select the **plus** sign.

Making Microsoft edge open to your favorite site

to add a page to your favorite place,

- Open Microsoft Edge and open the site you want to add
- Pick **Add this page to favorite** in the address bar
- You can rename the folder if you want to or choose another where you can save it.
- Select **done**

Revisiting favorite sites

To review a favorite site, simply open **edge** and click the **star**t/famous icon on the address bar, and you will immediately have access to your favorite pages

Finding things on the internet

Microsoft Edge uses **Bing search** to find a keyword on the internet. You can search from the search box on the **start menu,** and you can also do the same on the internet.

Saving info from the internet

Usually, most websites have a download button. When you download a file, they would be found on the **menu>downloads.**

Saving a webpage

You can save a webpage by adding it to favorites, or you can follow these steps to keep HTML

- Open the webpage on **edge.**
- Simultaneously click **alt + x** to bring the **settings** and **more** menu
- Go to **more tools> open with internet explorer**
- Go to **create a new folder** on the directory that you will use to save the web page content.
- In the **save as menu,** pick your preferred directory

Saving text

To save text, select it and copy it to keep it elsewhere.

Saving a picture

To download a picture, right-click on the image and select **save a picture** in the box that appears next.

Then a **save as** dialogue box will come next where you can select the directory that you want to keep your files in

Downloading a program, music, or any file

Most downloadable websites have icons that show that you can download from there. To download, click on that icon and follow the next step to choose a preferred directory. But remember to download only from trusted sites.

CHAPTER 10

NAVIGATING WINDOWS 11 PERIPHERALS: MAIL, CALENDAR, AND TEAMS CHAT

Having a good social life and teaming up with people for collaboration is tantamount to success in this day and age. Windows 11 fully supports this quest for collaboration. Here is how to link an account to team up with partners in windows 11 efficiently

Adding your accounts to windows

To add your account on users in windows:

- Go to the start menu
- And in the search box, type **computer management** and open it
- Add the account and password that you want to use
- And click create at the end of it.

Understanding the mail app switching among the mail app's views, menus, and accounts

The windows 11 mail application comes with a little more benefit than the windows ten application as it gives the users the option to add different types of accounts. Here is how windows 11 look like

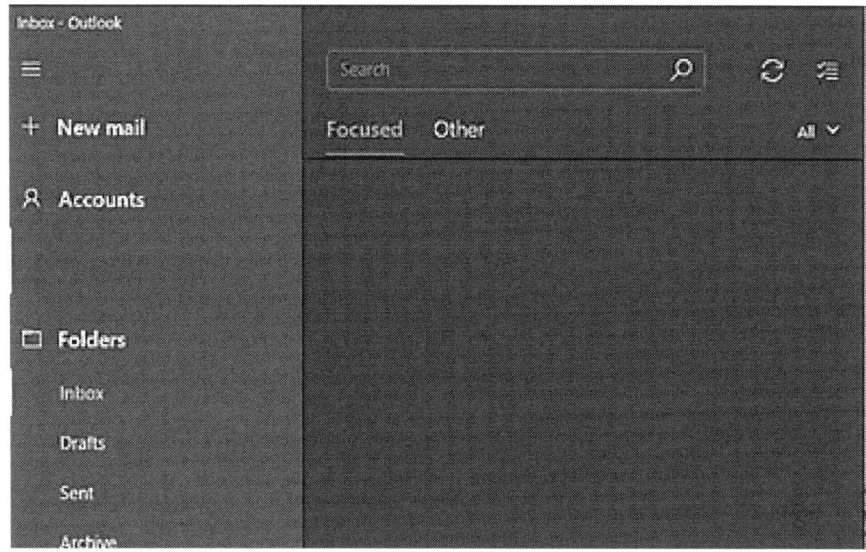

To add an **account** to the email, click **+add account,** and you will have some options to pick from. You can add, google, office 365, yahoo, iCloud, etc.

Composing and sending email

To compose and send a new email:

- Click new mail
- Type in the receiver email in**to**
- Then type in the **subject** of the email
- Type in the message of the email in the third text box
- And click **send** after reviewing all of the information within the email

Reading received email

If your email is open and your desktop is not on a metered network, then as far as you are online, you will be notified with any new email in the notification center. To read the email, go to the notification and tap it open. Then you can now read your new email

Sending and receiving files through email

to send a file through an email, then follow these steps:

- Go to **file explorer**
- Find the file
- Right-click on it
- Select **send to**
- Find **mail recipient** in the text box that comes next and select it

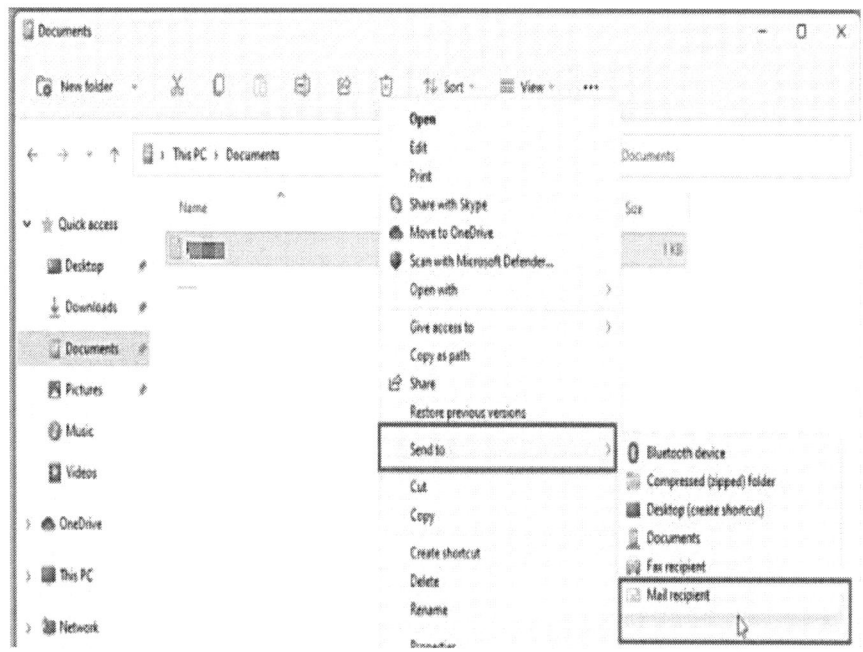

Managing your contacts in the people's app

The people's app is your windows address book. Here you can add a contact of people you know. The people app is synced with the mail and calendar, so you can easily traverse all of these.

Adding contacts

If you are opening the application for the first time,

- Click **get started**
- Give the people app access to your email by confirming the prompt

- Contacts in your logged-in account will be automatically synced to the people app. However, you can **import contacts**
- Finish by tapping **ready to go**
- Now, settings can't be found on the start menu; however, find this icon ⚇ in your email or outlook and open it.
- Go to **settings**

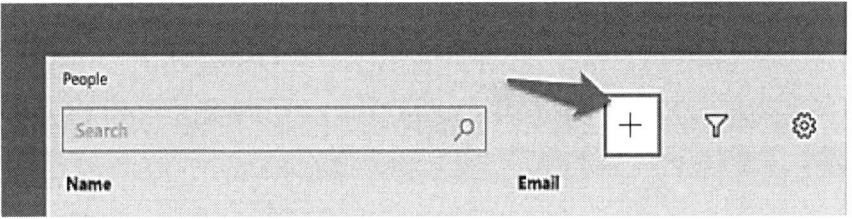

- **New contact+** follow the instructions that come next to add the account.

Deleting or removing contacts

When you delete a contact from the People app, then it will not be found in any other account you might have saved it in.

- Find the **people app**
- Use the search box to find the contact you intend to delete
- Use the **trash** 🗑 icon to

Managing appointments in calendar meeting online with team chat

```
📅 New meeting   Details   Scheduling Assistant

Time zone: (UTC-08:00) Pacific Time (US & Canada) ⌄

📅   Mar 10, 2020              4:00 PM  ⌄

     Mar 10, 2020              4:30 PM  ⌄    30m
```

- To book a meeting with people, pick **schedule a meeting (use the tiny calendar icon)**
- In the calendar, go to the top right and choose a **new meeting**
- Edit the time using the calendar

to invite people who are not in teams:
- With teams, **add required attendees.** and if you want someone to attend
- Add the person email
- Click **invite**. An email will be sent to the attendee with the link to the meeting embedded.

Starting team chat

To start a new chat, select **new chat** in the arrow on the image below

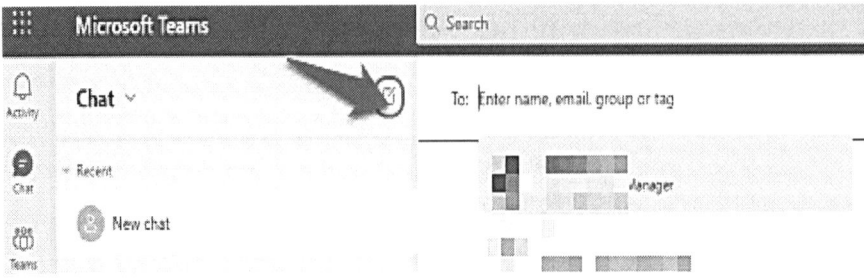

After selecting a **new chat,** enter the person's name and compose the message, then select the paper icon to send. Also, when you choose someone's profile card, you can send them a one-on-one chat

To start a group chat:

- Click **new chat**
- Add the preferred contacts to the field and then name the group in the **group name** field. Anyone within this group can send a message, and you can add as many as 250 people.

Sending a text message

Using the field provided on teams for conversation, you can send texts

Holding video chats

You can make a video call with team chats: you can just hover with your mouse above the contact, and a video icon will appear. Simply click it to start a chat.

64

CHAPTER 11
SAFE COMPUTING

It is important to remember t always stay safe once you are online. From hackers to fraudsters, there are a lot of people who want to do you harm once you are online. To know how to avoid all of these then you need t pay some attention to this chapter.

Understanding those annoying permission messages

There are a lot of permission messages on windows 11. Perhaps the one that comes out the most is the app permission messages. To manage this,

- Go to settings
- Then go to **privacy and security**
- Scroll down to **app permission** and once there, pick any permission list and give permission to any app you trust that requires them

Staying safe with windows security

Windows security is built-in software that is integrated with a windows defender—which is essentially an antivirus keeping your device and data safe right from the time you start your system. In the most recent installation, the updates are gotten automatically.

With the windows defender, you can:

- Protect your system from viruses and other threats
- All of your saved accounts are going to be safe
- An integrated firewall provides you with network protection from hackers
- You have more control over the apps
- Your device is safe, and the performance of your device is always going to be top-notch

Windows schedules when the defenders scan your device. However, you can always customize when you want it scanned by:
- In the **search box**, find the **task scheduler**
- In the subsequent pane, click **>** to highlight the **task scheduler library** and do the same thing with then open **Microsoft > windows,** then open the windows defender folder.
- In the tab that comes next, select **windows defender scheduled scan**
- When the action tab comes next, scroll to the bottom for **properties**
- In the next window, pick **trigger** then **new.**
- After choosing your preferred time, then you can select **okay.**

Avoiding and removing viruses

The windows defender is available to you at all times. However, there are a few people who do not trust the windows defender. Nevertheless, there are also a few trusted antiviruses that you can use like

- Avast;
- Quick heal;
- Etc.

Avoiding phishing scams

Phishing scams are when scammers try to use dubious means for you to give them your personal information. Sometimes, they look like companies you trust. However, you mustn't be tricked into giving them your information as they may have access to a host of other things with just your info like passwords and atm pins.

To protect yourself:

- Keep a security program running in your system
- Update your mobile phone regularly and run some security programs on it
- Protect all of your accounts using different credentials to authenticate them
- Back up all of your data

Setting up controls for children

Windows security provides an option for the family in other to protect your children's digital life to get her, open the **start menu>settings>update&security>windows security>family options**

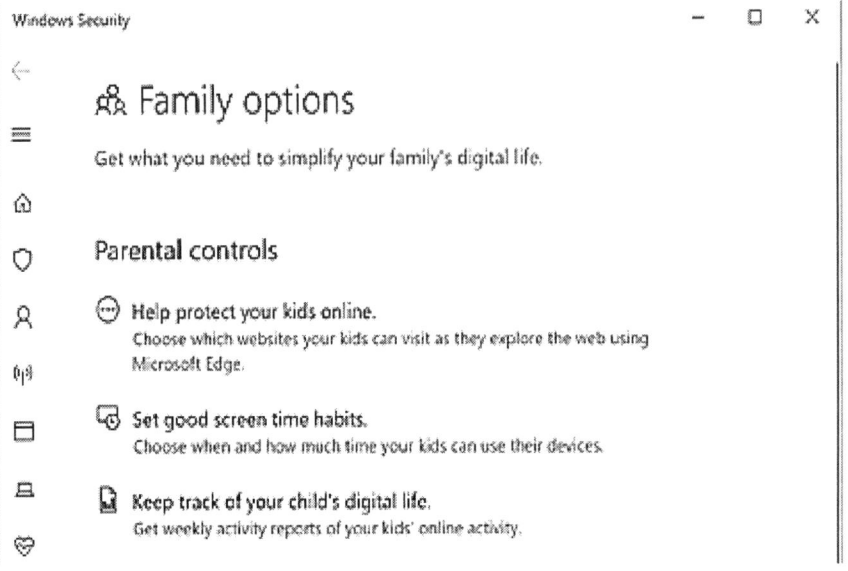

To manage your family settings, then go to **view family settings**

- Add a family member to an existing family or create one in the window
- You can get a report of your child's activity online
- Set your kid's screen time limit
- You can assign some money for your kid to shop with on the Microsoft store as you monitor what they spend the money on

CHAPTER 12

CUSTOMIZING SETTING IN WINDOWS

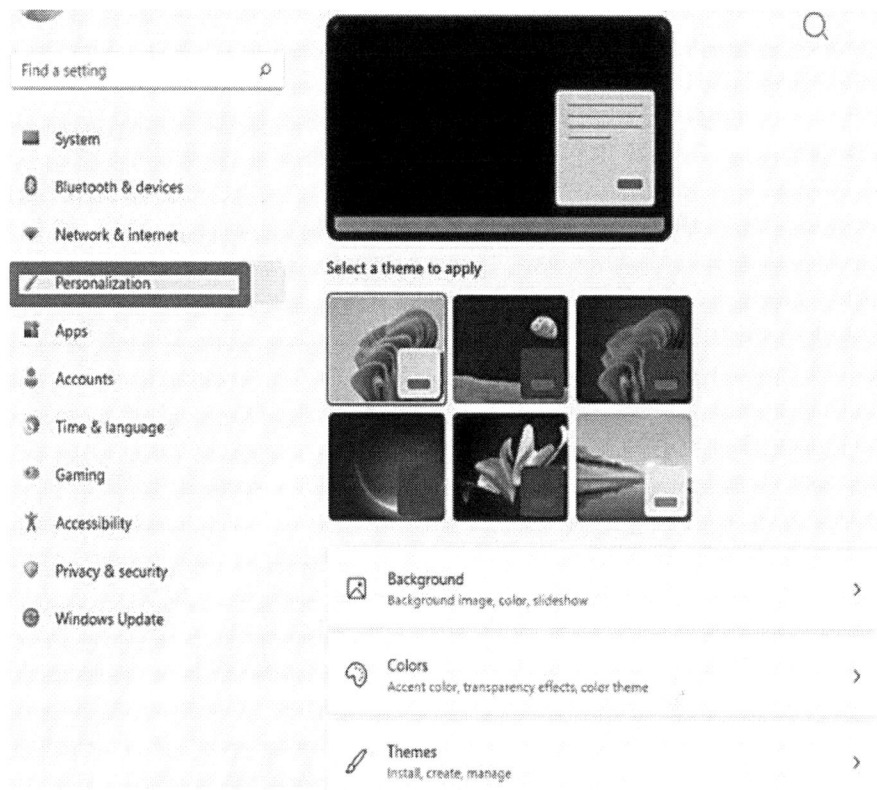

Finding the right switch

To get to the windows personalization setting, go to the **settings** on the **start menu.**

Adjusting the system settings

When in the system setting, you can adjust any setting you wish to. From personalization, security, network, etc.

Connecting and changing the Bluetooth and other devices.

- First, go to **settings**
- Then open the **Bluetooth** &**devices**
- Then select **add device** on the right pane

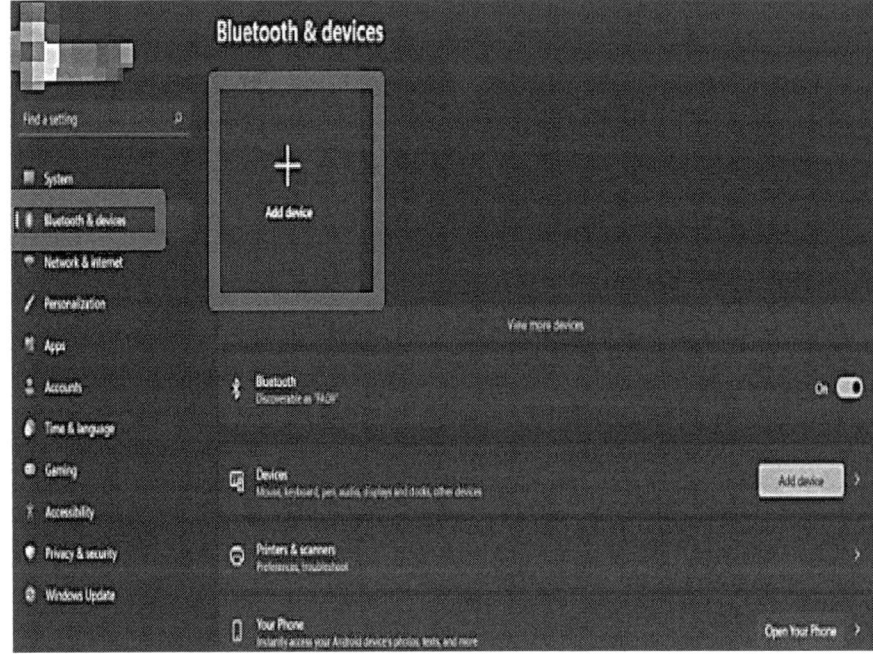

To transfer files:
- Go to **settings**>**Bluetooth** & **devices**
- Turn on your **Bluetooth**
- Select **view more devices** and navigate to **send and receive files via Bluetooth**
- Make your device visible.
- Follow all the instructions in the Bluetooth file transfer program that comes next.

Connecting to nearby wi-fi networks and the internet

- open **quick settings** on the bottom right of your taskbar

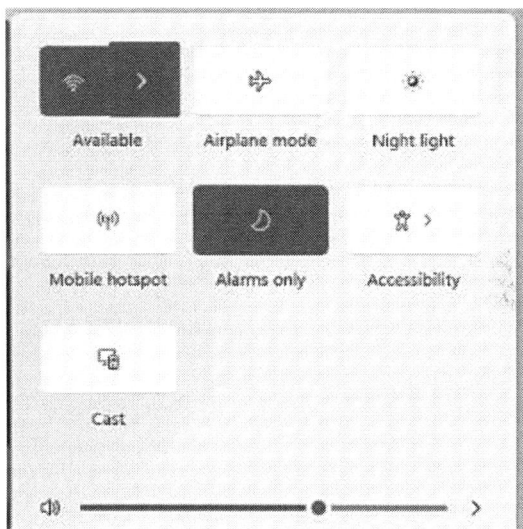

- Open **the wi-fi** icon

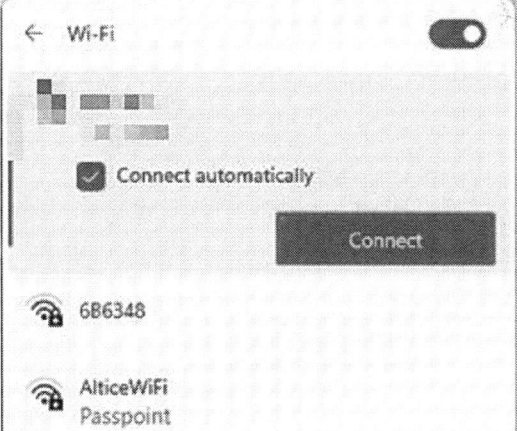

- Select **connect**

if there is any need to add a password, then you should find the option next

Personalizing your PC look and feel

All of the options to personalize your pc can be found in **start>setting>personalization.** Here you can control your pc background and color and take control of the aesthetics of your laptop.

Fixing and removing apps

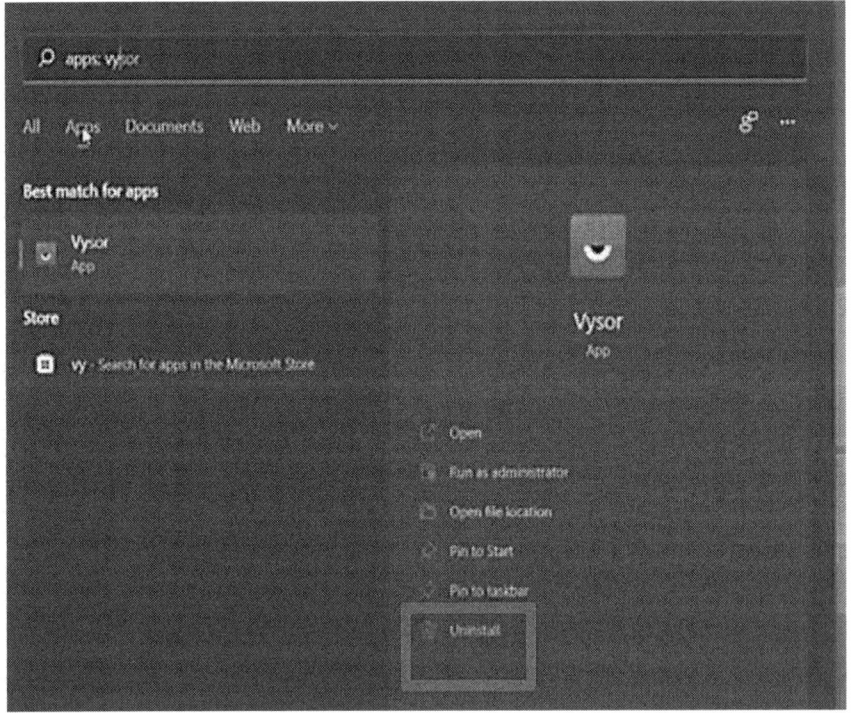

Windows 11 has made removing or uninstalling apps easy. You can simply search for an app on the start menu then

select uninstall in the option that comes below like the image above directs

Creating and changing accounts for others

- To create a new user account, navigate to **start>computer management>local users and groups>users>more action>new user**
- And select **create**

Changing date and time and language setting quickly

To change your time:

- Go to the system tray on the right-hand side of your system tray and right-click on the clock
- Pick adjust date and time option

Setting up for video games

Before playing a video game on pc, you must make your system run optimally. To add this setting;

- Go to the search bar on the start menu and search for **adjust the appearance and performance of windows.**
- In the tab that appears next, check to **adjust for best performance**
- Select **apply** and click **ok**

Adapting windows for your special physical needs

Accessing windows might not be easy for someone with special needs. This is why windows have thoughtfully upgraded the accessibility option. Here is how to adjust that.

On the windows, go to the **accessibility** option. Here you will find an option for anyone who needs them. they include aids for people who are having hearing and sight impairment

Managing your privacy and security

Accessing privacy and security is important as here you can have full access to your windows security and privacy. Got to **settings>privacy and security.**

Staying current and safe with windows update

in the windows 11 **settings>windows update**, you can check all of the available updates and patches. You can use the advanced option there to control the time that windows updates

CHAPTER 13

KEEPING WINDOWS FROM BREAKING

To most using windows, it is important that you have to keep all of your files safe and windows working smoothly. Here is one. Sometimes, the biggest threat to the safety of your files might not come from outside, but it might come from you. Here is how to keep your windows safe from you.

Back up your computer with file history

This is not an innovation as they have been introduced since the windows eight installation. Here is how to enable file history in windows 11

- Use the search box to look for **file history**
- Pick (**select drive**) in the following panel
- There you will find the list of the connected hard drive.
- After picking the preferred drive, then select **turn on**
- The system then begins to sync all the history of changes in your file

Finding technical information about your computer

- You can find out about your windows setting by searching **run** on the **search bar.**
- When the **run dialog** box opens, enter **winver** and select **ok**

Freeing up space on your hard drive

To free up space in your hard drive, use the cleanup recommendation feature on windows 11. Follow the following steps:

- Use the search box to find your **settings**
- go to storage on the right pane, and in the drop-down below, open **clean up recommendation**
- open it, and you will have access to four different categories of files you want to delete; temporary bin, files synced to the cloud, large or unused files, and uninstall apps.

This organization is the easy way out in case you are having trouble picking the right file to delete

Are you searching for storage detail?
To know your storage detail, simply follow the steps below:
- Go to **setting**
- **Scroll down and look for storage in the system area.**
- **Immediately, windows** will do a quick scan over all of the apps and the features in your system and show you how much each of the applications is using, like in your android application.
- you can also select **more categor**ies to see more of the applications that are not in the initial view

click on **apps** and **features**, and you will be provided with an app-by-app view of what is used

CHAPTER 14

SHARING ONE COMPUTER WITH SEVERAL PEOPLE

one of the benefits of windows is that you can share your computer with several people. Just create and link different users, and all of a sudden, you can collaborate, thereby facilitating smooth work

understanding user accounts

with the user account, you share one device with several people. What it does is tell windows which file each user can access and also what changes can be made on the computer from each user. The user system gives each person a separate password and different experiences on literally the same device

Adding an account for a family member or friend

Usually, you may want to share your device with someone you trust—that is family. So, to add a new user, follow the steps below:

To add a new account:

- Type **computer management** in the start menu search bar
- Go to **local users and group**
- Click **new users**
- Fill in the user name and password.

Changing existing accounts

simply use the **ctrl+alt+delete** to go to the switch user dialog windows. In the list, select **switch** user, and you will find a list of the available users on windows.

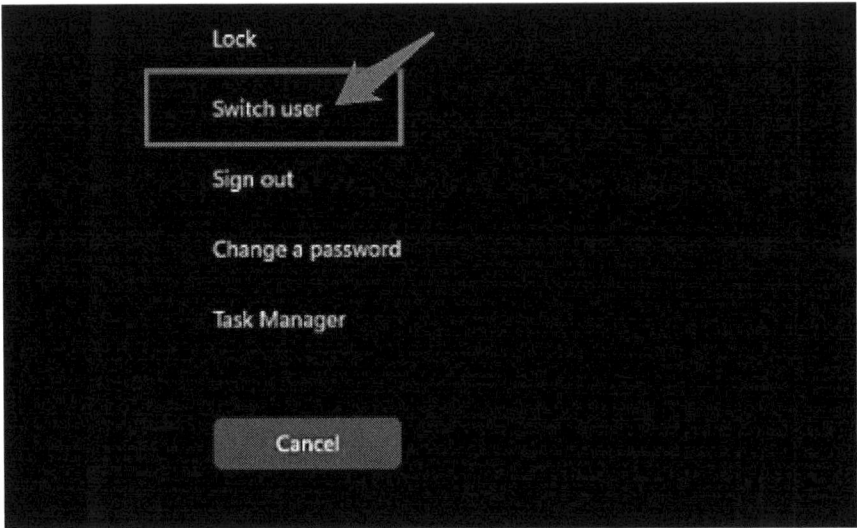

searching quickly between users

After following the step above, then you would have access to all of the available users, which you can switch to any of your choices.

Changing a user accounts picture

- Search for **setting** on the **start menu**
- Find **accounts**
- Select **your info**
- Adjust your photo by either taking one from the camera or a picture

Setting up password and security

- Go to **setting** on the **start menu**
- Then go to **your info.**
- **Then open password**

signing in with windows hello

- Sign in to your **Microsoft** windows account
- Go to **security**, then open **more security options**
- Go to **add** a **new way to sign in**
- Choose use windows PC
- Use the following dialog to open windows 11

CHAPTER 15

CONNECTING COMPUTERS WITH A NETWORK

To your computer has access to different modes of connecting to the internet. You can use an Ethernet cable, USB tethering, wi-fi, and modems.

Understanding a network part

Simply, a network connects you to the internet. There are three main parts:
- **The router:** which is a small box that controls information dissemination amongst the connected computers and the internet
- **The network adapter:** this network adaptor converts your systems radio signals and sends them to the router
- **Network cables:** if you are connecting wirelessly, then you do not need cables. However, if you're not, then you probably do not need this.

Setting up a small network

You have the choice to set up wired, wireless, and hybrid networks to connect your internet with printers and computer files.

Setting up a wireless router

- turn of ISP modem
- connect the Ethernet cable to LAN in your router

- connect from the router to Ethernet in your laptop the SSID or default passwords are usually on the sticker

Setting up Windows computers to connect to a network

You can use the quick setting on the bottom right side of the screen to swiftly connect to a wireless cable

Sharing files with your networked computer

- select the file you want to share and right-click on it. then select **give access to> specific people** in the menu

Setting your home network to private

- By default, your network will be in public mode. To change the got **settings** and open **network and wi-fi internet** and open **wi-fi**
- Open **manage known networks** then change the **wi-fi** network setting
- In-**network profile type** you can toggle between **public** or **private**

Sharing files and folders on your private network

You can share files over a network however you want to with the private network. The only difference is that your files will not be available to the public.

Accessing what others have shared

- Open your **file explorer**
- Open **network**
- You will see all the devices connected to you
- Then with any file shared with you, simply **double click**

Sharing a printer on the network

To share with a printer.
- Go to the control panel.
- Open your network and internet
- Go to the network and sharing center
- Switch the advanced sharing settings
- Go to the file and printer sharing part and turn it on

Sharing with nearby sharing

With nearby sharing, you can share copies of files, links, and more with devices that are close.

Turning on nearby sharing

Open your quick setting and toggle on your nearby sharing.

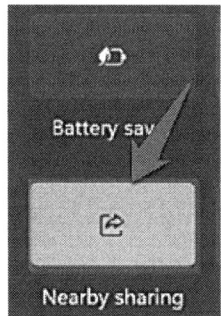

Sharing files with nearby sharing

- Open your file explorer.
- Right-click the file you want to share and select **show more option**
- Then select **share**
- Now you can share with **anybody who is nearby**

CHAPTER 16

PLAYING AND COPYING MUSIC

There are many possible applications that you can use to play and copy music in windows 11. You can go to the **Microsoft Store**; there you will find various options from the **groove music** application to the windows media player. There are a lot of options for you to choose from.

Playing music with the groove music app

The groove music application is an inbuilt application for windows 11. To use it to play your stored music:

- Use the **search box** on the **start menu** to search for the groove music application
- You will need to sign in to make purchases, however, if you have music stored in your music folder. However, you can add some other folders where it can read music from. To add a directory to choose music from, go to settings and tap the **add folder** button and follow all the instructions that follow.
- You have four different categories to search for music. They include the artist, album, playlist categories, and using the search box.

Handing music playing chores to windows

- You can use the search box to find the systems **control panel**
- Go to the **programs** tab

- Find **the windows media player** and set it as the **default** media player.

Stocking the windows media library

Here is how to add files to your windows media library
- Open the **organize** and select **manage libraries**. Here you will find a list of all the media files that can be played on windows media
- Choose the missing library, and select **add** then **ok** below.

Browsing the windows media libraries

The windows media library has all of the available media files available on your device given in four different categories, from music, videos, pictures to other media files.

Playing music files in the playlist

Your playlist is your personalized list of preferred music to listen to. When you open the windows media player, you will find the playlist category on the right-side pane of the windows media player.

Controlling your new playlist items

To add a song to your playlist, simply look for it using the search box and right-click on it, then select **add to** and pick your playlist.

Paying CDs

Immediately you add a CD to your device, the windows media player immediately recognizes it and pops up for you to play.

Playing DVDs

Just the same way the windows media plays CDs, so also does it play DVD. Just put the disk into your device in the CD-ROM space allotted to it. And immediately, it would start running. You can also have access to them through the file explorer.

Playing videos and TV shows

You can use the file explorer to find any video or tv show folder on your device. Nevertheless, windows media is capable of playing any video made for laptops and desktops

Creating, saving, and editing playlists

While you are on windows media

- find a song you want to add to a playlist and right-click on it,
- then select **add to**
- in the consequent dialog box, you will find the available playlist
- if you want a new playlist, then select a **new playlist** and type in your preferred name

Copying CDs into your pc

Copying a cd into your pc is as easy as copying folders within your pc. Just run the disk into your device and go to file explorer **CD ROM.** Once there, you can copy whatever the file is and paste them wherever you want to on your device by selecting them, then **right-clicking**, then selecting **copy** in the right-click option.

Burning (creating) CDs

To burn a CD, it has to be blank and readable.

- Find your media files and select **share** in the right-click tab
- Put your blank disk into your CD's disk tray.
- You can use the blank disk two ways, like a USB or as a CD
- Add a title for your disk
- Then choose **burn to disk** again

CHAPTER 17
FIDDLING WITH PHOTOS, VIDEOS, AND PHONES

It is nice to have all of your photos saved on your phone. However, do you know what it means for windows to help you organize it? Let's help you with that.

Copying photos from phones and camera

If your phone or camera has a USB port, then you can connect it with the pc. To do this, follow these steps.

- Unlock your phone can connect with your pc.'
- Open the photo app with the **start menu search box.**
- Follow the instructions after selecting **import from** the USB **device**

Making photos and videos with windows camera

- You can open cameras on your **search box**
- Then select the camera icon to take a photo or video icon to take a video (hover on the icons to be sure)
- Once you are done, all of your photos and videos will be saved on your pictures folder in file explorer.

Grabbing photos from your android phone with your phone app

Immediately you link your phone to your pc, and then you can use the application to see all of your photos that are in your android

Viewing collection of your photos

Go to your Photos app and select collection on the top panel

Viewing photo album

To find an album, select album on the photos app

Viewing slideshows

Select the slideshow icon on the photo app to make a slideshow

CHAPTER 18

TROUBLESHOOTING YOUR WINDOWS

This part deals with issues that you might face when using the windows 11

Resetting your computer

It eventually might become necessary to restore your desktop or laptop running windows 11 to the default setting. To do this:

- Go to **setting**
- Go to **system**
- On the right pane, click **recovery**
- When you open **recovery**, select **reset pc**
- If you want to keep all **your files** or **remove everything**, choose your preference and continue
- Pick your option of resetting windows—cloud download or local reinstall
- Click **next**
- Then select **reset**

Restoring backups with files history

To restore a backup with the file history,

- Attach your external storage with the backup
- Open the control panel with the search box
- One the control pane, search for file history

- Then choose to save backup copies of the file with file history
- Then go along with the instructions that follow

Windows keep asking me for permission

To stop windows from asking you for approval,

- Open your control panel with the search box
- Go to **system and security**
- Then **security and maintenance**
- Look for the **windows smart screen section**
- Choose change setting
- Here you can tell windows what to do with unknown apps

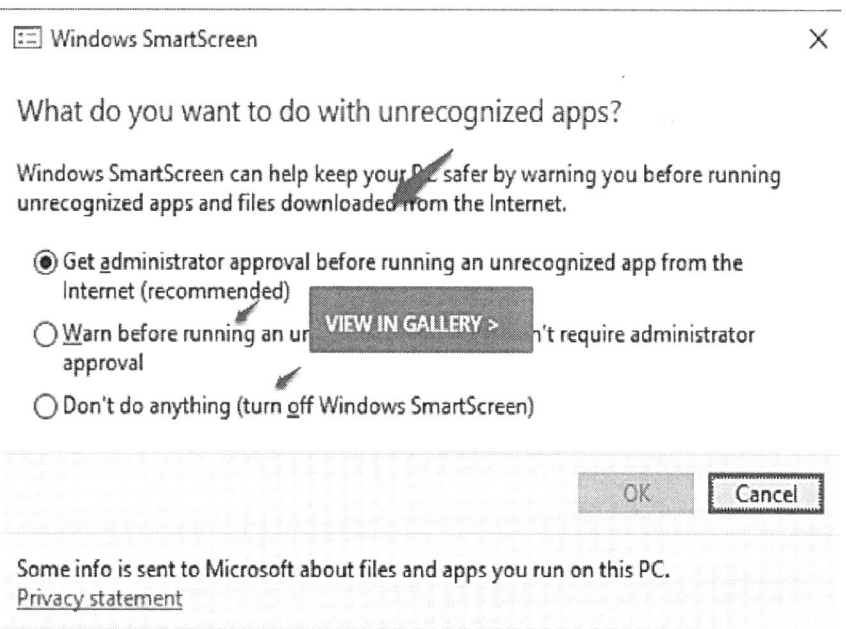

Retrieving deleted files

You can find all the deleted files in your **recycle bin** folder, usually by default at the top right corner of your desktop screen. To restore a file, double click on it or select it and right click then select the **restore** option in the dialogue box that follows.

I need to fix broken apps

To troubleshoot an application, make sure that your window is up to date. You can troubleshoot applications from the Microsoft store by:

- Going to the **library** on **Microsoft store**
- Choose to **Get updates**

My settings are messed up

 To reset your settings, follow the factory reset step given in this chapter, but when you get to the option to remove everything or keep all of your files, select **keep all your files.**

I forgot my password

 If you forget your password and cannot find a way into your computer, don't worry, there is a way to do this.

- In the sign-in screen, select reset **password**
- Answer your security question
- Add anew password

Frozen computer

There are many ways to restart a frozen computer; you can use the **Esc** button or the task manager to end the task of freezing your laptop. However, sometimes it usually gets awful to the point where you might need a hard restart by holding your system's power button for over 3 to 4 seconds. The hard restart, however, is not recommended unless you have tried all the other available options.

CHAPTER 19

STRANGE MESSAGES ON YOUR PC

Add Microsoft account

Whenever you see this message, it means you do not have a Microsoft account logged into the device, and you probably need to

Calendar notification

Here you will find notifications, reminders, and tasks to do

Choose what happens with this device

To choose what happens with this device, you probably have connected your pc with a different device. You have the option to select from a range of possible options or ways you can use the device through your laptop; it is attached to

Deleted files are removed everywhere

This means that you do not want the file stored in the recycle bin for a while, and you also don't want them backed up to the cloud. So, a file deleted this way is going to be lost entirely.

Did you mean to switch apps?

This occurs when you have switched apps suddenly, and your device notices it. so it asks

Do you want to allow this app to make changes to your device?

This happens when an app writes or changes settings or files on your device. To accept this, make sure that you trust the app and review what you are consenting to

Do you want to save changes?

Usually, this happens before you exit a file. Say yes to keep the changes and select no not to save the changes.

Enter network credential

Network credentials might include passwords and settings

How do you want to open these files?

Depending on the various possible ways a file may be opened, you can decide to open the app with different options.

Keep these display settings

This has to do with the way a screen is displayed on a window; usually, you want to keep it to be used to that.

Let's finish setting up

To finish, select **yes** or **no**

No usable drive Found

This happens when you are trying to back up a file to an external drive. If the drive is not connected correctly, then it tends to give you this error message.

Save to one drive

OneDrive, cloud-based storage, backs up all your file. So when you save to them, you are backing them up to the cloud

Select to choose what happens with removable drives

This happens when you connect an external device, and there are many possible ways to use that device on your laptop or desktop.

Threat found

Threats may include harmful bugs in your system. Windows defenders and many other antiviruses are capable of finding and nullifying threats to your computer

USB device not recognized

This happens with bad USBs or when the USB is not properly connected

Verify your id on this pc

To verify your id, you need to submit your credentials

We are not allowed to find you

This means that Windows does not monitor your location

You do not have permission to access this folder

This means that the folder is either sensitive and not writeable, or it is locked from you.

Your privacy setting blocked access to the location

This happens when you add a privacy setting. This way, your location will not be turned on or public

CHAPTER 20

MOVING FROM OLD PC TO NEW WINDOWS 11 PC

Eventually, you would have to move from one pc to the other. Here is how to do this

Moving to Windows 11, the Microsoft way

Earlier in this book, we have already told you how to restore all your settings from an old pc to your new windows 11 pc

Having a third party to make the move

There are ways to add a new user, which have already been discussed earlier.

Buying lap links pc mover programs

Laplink moves all your applications, files, and setting. This program will help you save settings. when you run it, it assists you with the necessary details to restore all your settings

Visiting a repair shop

When you visit a repair shop, be sure that you are in a trusted and certified shop as many quack repairmen will take your device and return it worse than it was when you brought it

Transferring files yourself

you can personally transfer files by choosing to move them with an external hard drive or another possible way you can

CHAPTER 21

HELP ON THE WINDOWS HELP SYSTEM

It can be great to get help, and Microsoft provides one. here is how to reach out

getting started with windows 11

immediately you install windows, you immediately get instructions on how to get started to review the instruction, and if you are not clear, then contact Microsoft support

Contacting support

Microsoft support options

To get Microsoft support, go to support. You or Microsoft.Com can call 012710156

Microsoft free support option

Microsoft support service is free; however, if you are making calls, airtime or data charges may be incurred

CHAPTER 22

TEN THINGS YOU WILL HATE ABOUT WINDOWS 11 AND HOW TO FIX THEM

Knowing whether your PC can upgrade to Windows 11

Microsoft has created a very strict system requirement for whichever system is going to be operating Windows 11. This is particularly surprising as most modern systems would have no problem operating it.

The operating system that is allowed to run windows 11 is specific. It would be best if you had at least a 7th generation intel core or AMD plus the second generation ryzen processor and a 4gig ram with at least 64 gig storage space, TPM 2.0, and finally, it has to support secure boot.

Looking at this requirement, we want to understand that it is strict. Nevertheless, the only reason why it is so is to maximize the safety of the user, and it is only computers that already have these features that can enjoy all of the benefits of windows 11. It is basically like a ps5 without a 4k television. You might still play it without the 4k television. But the only way your experience is going to be different from the ps4 experience is when you use a 4k television.

Microsoft understands that it is important to maintain reliability over a period, which usually implies **OEM and IHV** driver support. With these drivers, it is easier for Microsoft to manage the windows update in a coordinated fashion. And there is a better system that checks the device's health. With this, the reliability of the system with windows 11 is improved upon.

A trusted and **secure boot** is one requirement that is important to download windows 11. For systems integrated with secure boots which need both **UEFI** and **TPM hardware**, the damage is minimal when the system is compromised. These two requirements ensure that hackers cannot gain access to your **bootkits** and **rootkits** and edit them.

Also, why the requirements are so strict is due to the high demands of windows 11 to run on devices. Systems that are not supported by windows 11 are 52% more susceptible to kernel crashes. And this is the most important information to the user as they will have more peace of mind not installing windows 11 with unsupported devices. In contrast, supported devices are only likely to crash 0.2% of the time.

Finally, performance is going to be a problem with older devices trying to run windows 11; according to some tests run by Microsoft on older hardware, older hardware is not compatible and can become disastrous to your device health and even your overall user experience with windows.

There is no backup program

You can restore files with backup and restore. To do this

- Attach the external drive with your backup
- Go to the control panel by looking for it through the start menu search box.
- Choose backup and restore (windows7)
- Choose another backup where you want to restore files and select the directory of your external storage, then follow the subsequent instructions.

I want the start button and menu in the lower-left corner.

The first thing that you are going to observe with windows 11 is that the start menu is on the center of the screen instead of the left side. You can live it that way. But, for people like us who prefer things to stay the same traditionally, we expect that it should be left on the left side of the screen. Here is how to move it to the left side of the screen.
- Open your **windows setting.**
- Find the **personalization and go to the taskbar.**
- Find **taskbar alignment** where the **taskbar behavior** is
- Pick the **left** side in the drop-down that follows

Windows 11 keeps changing

Windows generally do not change.

I don't want a Microsoft account

You can set up windows 11 without a Microsoft account. When you are setting it up, just put your system in airplane mode and disconnect the cable when you get to the license agreement part. After doing that then you can create a local account instead of a Microsoft account

Windows makes me sign in all the time

To remove the windows, sign in:

- Open settings windows
- Go to the **accounts** and find **ways to sign in**
- Select **password** and select **change**
- Add your password, then click next and make sure that you make sure every field is empty, then select **finish.**

I can't line up two windows on the screen

To line up two windows on your screen. Hold the window with your mouse from the middle of the tab and push it to a side of the screen till the windows tab will not go in anymore and release it. Then you will find that windows will be on one side of the screen.

It won't let me do something unless I'm an administrator

Usually, it would be best if you had the windows administrator for extra security for your programs and device health. Select **yes** to continue

I don't know what version of windows I have

- To know your window version, find **computer** on your start screen
- Right-click on computer
- Then open **properties** and go to windows edition

My print screen key does not work

- You can restore background programs like one drive, snippet, and dropbox if they are preventing your print screen from working.
- Open the task manager with the hotkeys **ctrl +shift +esc**
- Then right-click on these programs and choose **the end task** to close it.

CHAPTER 23

TIPS FOR TABLET AND LAPTOP OWNERS

Using the new touchscreen gesture

To enable gestures then you can go to the **settings>Bluetooth and devices> touch three and four-finger touch gestures**, then turn it on. There are various gestures to optimize your experience with windows 11

Switching to airplane mode

You can use the **quick setting** option on the right-hand side of the screen to switch on and put off airplane mode. Just select the airplane icon on the quick setting to put it on and off

Connecting to a new wireless internet network

- open **quick settings** on the bottom right of your taskbar

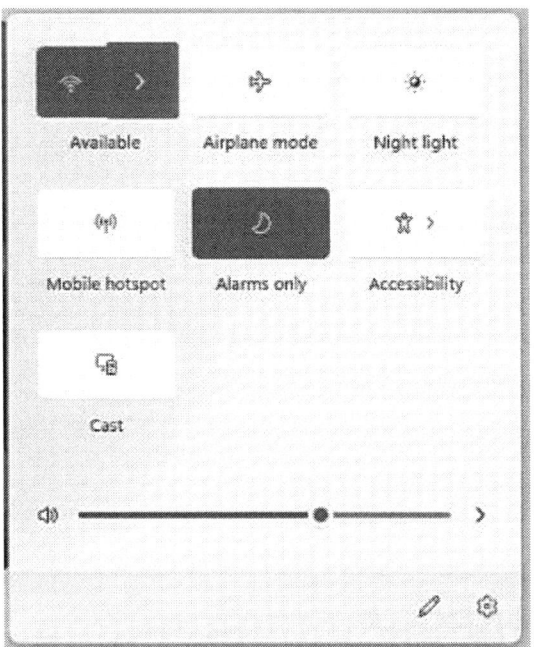

- Open **the wi-fi** icon

- Select **connect**
  if there is any need to add a password, then you should find the option next

Toggling your tablet screen rotation

- Right-click anywhere on the desktop and select **display setting**
- Look for **display orientation**
- Find any design you want and select it
- You can confirm any change by selecting the keep changes button

Adjusting to a different location

- Open **setting>privacy>location**
- Under the default location, choose set default
- Then go along with the instructions to change the default location in the map that appears next.

Turning on the traffic widget

Traffic widget comes with the widgets, which are by default on the Windows 11 start menu.

Accessing the mobility center

Hold the **win+x,** and you will find **a mobility center.** Simply select it to open it.

Backing up your laptop before traveling

It can be necessary to back up your laptop in an external drive using the file history.

Turning calculator into a road warrior tool

To turn the calculator on, simply go to the search box on the start menu and search for a calculator and select it to open it. You can use it to calculate dates, convert currencies, convert volumes, length, weight, and mass, temperature, energy. Etc.

CHAPTER 24
DISK MANAGEMENT

How to manage disk and drive storage setting

When you are low on space or for whatever reason only known to you, feel that you need to free up some space or generally just want to manage your drive storage, Windows 11 lets you do this. Here is what you want to do to free up some space in your windows.

- Go to **setting**
- **Scroll down and look for storage in the system area.**
- **Immediately, windows** will do a quick scan over all of the apps and the features in your system and show you how much each of the applications is using, like in your android application.
- You can also select **more categor**ies to see more of the applications that are not in the initial view
- click on **apps** and **features**. You will be provided with an app-by-app view of what is used
- but if you go back and click on the **temporary files, you** will have the option to simply just removes all the files by clicking on the **remove files.** Usually, from time to time, due to the space utilized, it will be necessary to do this. Be sure that you **check** and **uncheck** the preferred files that you want to remove

Clean Up the Recommendation

Go to the **settings>storage>clean up recommendations** Here you are going to find all the recommendations that windows have for you to clean. this is helpful as it will provide those applications that you are not using or videos and files that you have forgotten but are just clogging up your drive and is bringing you into the position where you have to free up some space

Storage sense

In the **system>storage>storage sense**. You will have an innovation here that makes you stress less and reduces the times when you have to manage the systems space. By checking the **automatic user content cleanup**, you will have the windows Ai do that for you.

You can also edit the setting under it so that it knows when to delete anything that needs deleting. You have the option to delete **every day, week, or month.**

Furthermore, you have the option to set the times you want to clean up your recycle bin. If you want to clean the recycle bin daily, or weekly, or monthly, then you can do that.

Finally, files that have not been opened for a long time will be deleted here when you approve a setting. By default, it never deletes. However, you can change the setting to delete within one month or a day.

Are you searching for storage detail?

To know your storage detail, simply follow the steps below:

- Go to **setting**
- **Scroll down and look for storage in the system area.**
- **Immediately, windows** will do a quick scan over all of the apps and the features in your system and show you how much each of the applications is using, like in your android application.
- you can also select **more categor**ies to see more of the applications that are not in the initial view
- click on **apps** and **features**, and you will be provided with an app-by-app view of what is used

Increasing decreasing the partition size of the drive

Just like Windows 10, Windows 11 comes with a native disk management tool. Here, it not only deletes, creates, and formats partitions; however, you can also change the allocated partition and not lose data. Nevertheless, the disk management tool is not the most efficient tool to change the size of the windows 11 partition. The disk management tool in Windows 11 can only be used to decrease partition, delete or increase the size of the partition. However, the windows 11 disk management tool cannot increase volumes of partitions by shrinking another.

Here is how to decrease partition sizes on your drive

- Click both the **Windows + X** key and then open the disk management
- Any of the NTFS partitions you want to click can be shrunk if you right-click them
- Enter a space amount and then enter the shrink button. Without entering an amount but by default, it is going to use as much space as it can

How to increase the size of the windows 11 partition

here is how to increase the windows 11 partition:

- after opening the disk management as referred to in the items above,
- move the files from the right area to other places
- right-click this partition and pick delete volume. Immediately disk space is going to be unallocated
- right-click the left contiguous like C: then pick **extend volume**
- then follow the **extend volume wizard** that pops up

CHAPTER 25

WINDOWS KEYBOARDING

The keyboard is one of the input devices of a computer system. It is the device we use to send data and information to the computer. It is made up of different keys which are the Alphanumeric keys, Navigation keys, Control keys, and Function keys. The keyboard is an easy way of communicating with the computer.

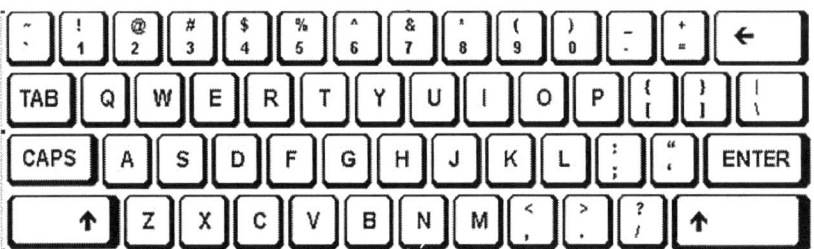

How to change your keyboard settings on windows 11

- Click on the **Search icon** on your taskbar.
- Type in Control Panel. Click on the **Control Panel** option

- Select **Keyboard**. The Keyboard Properties menu pops up.

- You can now change your Keyboard settings such as **The Character Repeat delay, the Repeat rate,** and **The Cursor blink rate.**

How to add a keyboard layout on windows 11

Windows 11 operating system allows its users to customize multiple keyboard layouts. It also allows you to change, add and delete layouts. We will guide you on the steps to change, add and delete keyboard layouts.

To add a keyboard layout, simply follow the outlined steps below;

- Open up your **Start** menu and search for **Settings.**

- On your setting window, search for **Keyboard** and select the **Edit Language and Keyboard option**

- Click on the **three dots** next to your default language.

- Select **Language options**. Under Keyboards, click on **Add a Keyboard.**

- This allows you to add a new keyboard layout for your operating system.

How to delete a keyboard layout on windows 11

- Click the **Windows Start button** and select **Settings**
- Click on **Time and Language** and select **Language & Region**
- Click on the keyboard layout you want to remove. Then, select **Remove**

How To Change Keyboard Layouts on Windows 11

- Right-click on your **Windows Start** button. Then, click on **Settings.**

- On the left-hand side, select the **Time and Language Settings**.

- Click on the **Language & Region** section. Here, you will see all the languages which are supported by your Windows 11 operating system.

- You will have a default display language for your keyboard probably **English (United Kingdom).**
- You can add any language you wish to add by clicking on the **Add a language** option.

- Select the language you want to add. Then, click on **Next.**

- Click on **Install**. After the installation, the language you selected will be added.
- On the right-hand side of your taskbar, is your **language input indicator**. Click on it, you will see the added language on the keyboard layout window.

- By clicking on the icon, you can now change your keyboard layout and switch between the keyboard layouts.

How to activate the language input indicator on windows 11

The language Input Indicator is a system icon that appears on the right-hand side of the taskbar. It appears when you add a keyboard layout or a new language. It makes it easy for you to switch keyboard layouts without making use of settings. To activate the input indicator, kindly follow the steps listed below;

- Click on the **Search** icon on your taskbar. Search for **Settings**.

- Click on settings and select **Personalization.**

- On the left-hand side, click on **Taskbar**. Scroll down to the **Notification area option**. Under the notification area option, click on **Turn system icons on or off**.

- On the prompt, you will find the **Input indicator** option. Turn it **ON**.

- The language input indicator will appear on the right-hand side of your taskbar. When it is turned off, the Input Indicator will disappear from the taskbar.

Windows 11 New Keyboard Shortcuts

On Windows 11 operating system, Microsoft added new keyboard shortcuts that will help its users work faster and more efficiently. Below are the newly introduced keyboard shortcuts on Windows 11;

1. **Windows key + W**= This opens the Widgets interface.

2. **Windows key + A** = This opens the Action Center. The Action Center is located at the lower right-hand side of the taskbar. From there, you can visit your setting page from the quick setting shortcut icon. On it, you can also access your Bluetooth, Airplane mode, Focus assists, etc.

3. **Windows key + C** = This opens Microsoft Teams.

4. **Windows key + N** = This opens the Notification Panel. The notification panel is where you see all your notifications on the computer.

5. **Windows key + Z** = This opens Quick Access to Snap Layout.

How to enable the touch screen keyboard on windows 11

The touch screen keyboard is the keyboard that appears on the screen of your computer. It allows you to input text into the computer by tapping on the keyboard either with your mouse or your fingertip. When you enable the touch screen keyboard, it will remain on the screen of your computer till you close the application. To enable the touch screen keyboard on Windows 11, simply follow the steps outlined below;

- Click on the **Start** menu. Then select **Settings.**
- Click on **Personalization**.

- On the left-hand side, click on the **Taskbar** option.
- On the prompt, you will find the **Show Touch Keyboard** option. Turn it **ON.**

- The Touch-Screen keyboard will appear.

How to enable the touch screen keyboard using the ease of access center

- Click on the **Windows Start** menu. Click on **Settings.**
- Click on the **Ease of Access** option.
- Select **Keyboard**. Then, on the Touch Screen Keyboard option, **Turn ON** the toggle.

Clipboard

The Clipboard is a location on a computer system where information or data that are copied or cut are stored. When you copy or cut something, it is automatically stored in the clipboard. You can transfer your cut or copied information from one application to another. This means that when you store data or information on a clipboard, you can paste it to a new location.

You can store lots of data on the clipboard but this depends on the **physical memory (RAM)** of the computer. If the RAM of the computer is high, then you can store a lot of data on the clipboard. The clipboard can store files such as images, texts, files, or other types of data.

How to enable clipboard history on windows 11

Enabling clipboard history allows you to have multiple items saved to your clipboard at once. When you copy something(s) on your PC, they are stored in your clipboard history. If you want to copy and paste something and have it saved to the clipboard, you will have to enable your clipboard history first, and to do that, follow the steps below;

- Right-click on the **Start** button. Select **Settings.**
- Select **System.**
- Scroll down on the right-hand side and select **Clipboard.**
- Turn **ON** the toggle switch beside the **Clipboard History** option.
- You can view your clipboard history and paste from it by pressing the **Windows key** and **V key** at the same time. The clipboard history menu will appear on the right-hand side of the taskbar.

You can also remove items from your clipboard history. You can do this using the steps below;

- Click on the **Windows Start** menu icon and select **Setting**.
- In the settings window, select **System setting**.
- Scroll down on the right-hand side and select **Clipboard.**

- On the clear clipboard data option, click on **Clear.**

You can easily get to your clipboard history by pressing the Windows Key + V.

How to use paste as plain text from clipboard history on windows 11

When using the paste as plain text option in clipboard history, the text you copied will be pasted without its original formatting (size, color, font). It allows the text to be in line with the formatting of the destination documents. You can use the paste as plain text from the clipboard by following the steps below;

- Open your Clipboard history. You can simply do this using the shortcut key **(Windows key + V).**
- Click on the **Three dots** button next to the content you want to paste.

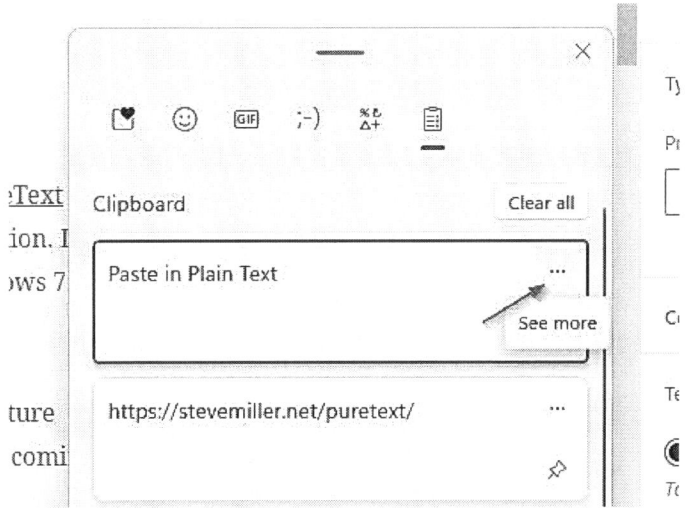

- Click on The **Paste as Text** option. The text you selected will be pasted as plain text with no formatting.

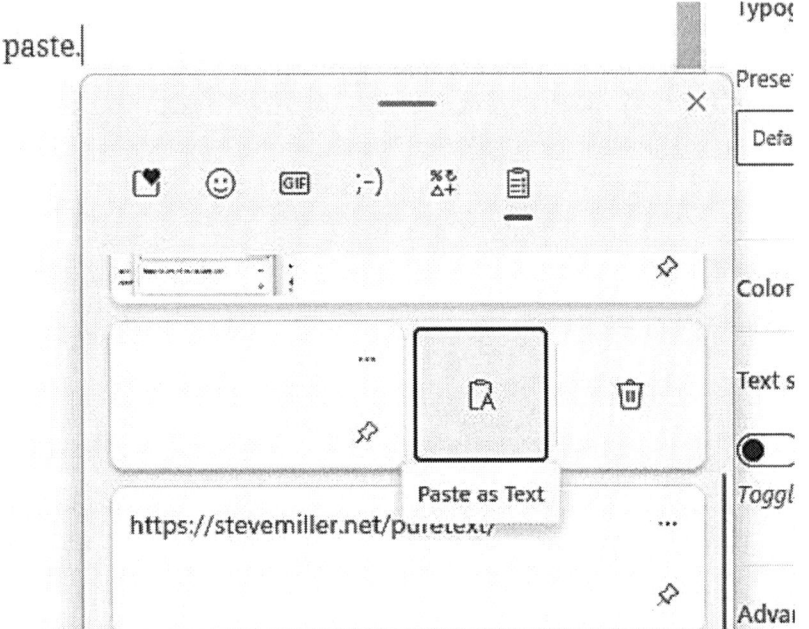

CHAPTER 26
WINDOWS FONT

Fonts

Fonts are graphical representation of text that includes a different typeface, point size, weight, color, or design. It is a specific size and variation such as bold or italic. They are used to add style and design to a document. The use of different fonts for different applications started way long ago even before the advent of digital world processing. Fonts are in different forms; you can make use of different fonts in your works. Changing fonts back then was done by changing metallic movable type, just like in a typewriter or printing press. Fonts improve the readability and legibility of your works whether documents or designs.

How to download and install fonts on windows 11

- Download the font you want from the **Web**. When the font is downloaded, it comes in a zip file.

- Go to your Download menu. **Right-click** on the zip file and click on **Extract All**.

- Once the files have been extracted, right-click on the font you want to install and select **Install for all users.**

- Now the font has been installed.

You can also add fonts on Windows 11 using Settings. To do this, simply follow the outlined procedures below;

- Click on the **Windows Start menu** on your taskbar. Select **Settings**.

- On the prompt, search for **Font Settings.**

- On the right-hand side of the menu, you will see the **Add Fonts option** which indicates **"Drag and drop to install"** in the box below it. You can drag font files from your file explorer or your desktop and drop them in the box.

- On the **Available fonts** option, you can search for the fonts you want to install or you select from the list of the available fonts presented to you.

How to change your default font style on windows 11

The default font style on Windows 11 operating system is Segoe UI Variable. It is a new version of the classic Segoe and uses variable font technology. Segoe UI enhances high legibility and readability in the User Interface. You may not like the font and would like to change it; you can follow the steps below to do so;

- Click the **Windows Start menu** on your taskbar. On the search box, search for **Notepad**.
- When the Notepad window opens, type in the following;

Windows Registry Editor Version 5.00

[HKEY_LOCAL_MACHINE\SOFTWARE\Microsoft\Windows NT\CurrentVersion\Fonts]
"Segoe UI (TrueType)"=""
"Segoe UI Bold (TrueType)"=""
"Segoe UI Bold Italic (TrueType)"=""
"Segoe UI Italic (TrueType)"=""
"Segoe UI Light (TrueType)"=""
"Segoe UI Semibold (TrueType)"=""
"Segoe UI Symbol (TrueType)"=""
[HKEY_LOCAL_MACHINE\SOFTWARE\Microsoft\Windows NT\CurrentVersion\FontSubstitutes]
"Segoe UI"="FONT-STYLE"

Once you are done typing in the above content, do not close the Notepad window, you can minimize it.

- Then, click on the **Windows Start** menu and select **Settings**.
- Click on **Personalization**, then select **Fonts**.
- On the lists of the available fonts, choose the font style you want. Then copy the name.
- Go back to the Notepad page. Replace the **FONT STYLE** with the font name you just copied.
- Click on **File**, then click on **Save as**.
- In the saving pop-up menu, select the location where you want to save the file, put in the name of the file, and while naming the file add **.reg** at the end of the file name. Then, click **Save**.

- Now, go to the location you have saved the file, **double-click** on it to open it. Click **Yes** on the prompt that appears on your screen. Then, click **Ok**.

- **Restart** your computer.

To restore your default font settings, simply

- Click on the **Search icon** on your taskbar and search for the **Control panel**.

- Click on **Appearance and Personalization**. Then, select **Fonts**

- Click on **Change Font Settings**. On the menu, you will see the **Restore default font settings option.** Click on it.

To change your font size on Windows 11, all you have to do is:

- Click on the **Start menu** and select **Settings**.
- Click on **Accessibility**. Then, click on **Text size.**

- On the Text size preview page, you will see a slider. You can adjust the slider to the left and to the right to change the size of the font of your computer. Adjusting it to the left makes the fonts get smaller while adjusting to the right makes the fonts get bigger.

- Click on **Apply**.

PRIMARY MONITOR ON WINDOWS 11

The primary monitor is the monitor that your computer displays everything on. It is the main monitor of your computer. On your PC, you can have more than one monitor connected to it. All the Microsoft Windows Operating Systems support dual monitors and multiple displays. When you have more than one monitor on your PC, one of the monitors will work as the primary monitor (this is usually the first monitor that was connected to your computer) and the other will serve as the external monitor. You can also choose which monitor you would like to be your primary monitor and the one to serve as the external monitor.

How To Change The Primary Monitor Of Your Computer

- Click on the **Windows Start menu** and select **Settings**. You can also use the **Windows key + I** shortcut keys to open settings.
- On the left-hand side of the Settings menu, click on **System**.
- Click on **Display**. Then, click on **Multiple Displays**. This will display your monitors. You can click on the **Detect** option to detect other monitors on your computer if any.
- Click on the icon of the monitor you want to make your main display. Then, click on the box on the **Make this my main display** option.
- You can also drag and drop the monitors from left to right.

CHAPTER 27

WINDOWS 11 AS A VIRTUAL MACHINE

What is a virtual machine?

A Virtual Machine is a software. It is like another computer inside a computer. Like we all know that software is a set of programs that tells a computer what to do, it makes a computer easy to use, for example like Windows, Mac OS X, Linux, Android, and IOS. Here, a Virtual Machine is that software that allows us to run more operating systems within an existing operating system. With a virtual machine, you can install any operating system, install whatever application you want on your computer. Examples of Virtual Machines are VirtualBox and VMware. When you install Virtualbox on your computer, you can have two virtual machines. One with Windows 8 and the other with Windows XP. You can now use these two virtual machines as if they were real computers. You can use a virtual machine when you want to test an application or when you are trying a new operating system.

Advantages of virtual machines

- With the use of virtual machines, you can run many operating systems at the same time on your computer.
- Virtual machines enhance the security of the data and information on your computer.
- They are so reliable. The machines might spoil or crash but nothing will happen to the host computer.

- They help test your applications to identify any virus to prevent it from affecting the computer.
- Virtual machines increase the efficiency and productivity of your computer.

How does a virtual machine work?

Virtualization is the process in which virtual machines work. A computer server often referred to as the host machine is separated into smaller guest machines through a process called Virtualization. This process is managed by a hypervisor. A hypervisor is a software that creates and runs virtual machines. It allows the host machines to run multiple virtual machines, of which each of them might be running different operating systems. Each of the virtual machines behaves like it was its computer because it has its operating system and storage. When the virtual machines are not running, they are stored as images. The images are a collection of files that serves as a template for reproducing the virtual machine. You can manage virtual machines on both your computer and other computers.

How to create a virtual machine on windows 11

To set up your virtual machines, you will need a software called a hypervisor to do that. You will have to check if your computer is compatible with the requirements to run a hypervisor on Windows 11. To be able to run a hypervisor, you need either Windows 10 professional or enterprise, an x64 based PC. You can follow the outlined procedures to check your system's compatibility;

- Click on the **Search icon** on your taskbar. Search for **Command Prompt**.

- Right-click on it and select **Run as administrator**. Then, click **Yes**.

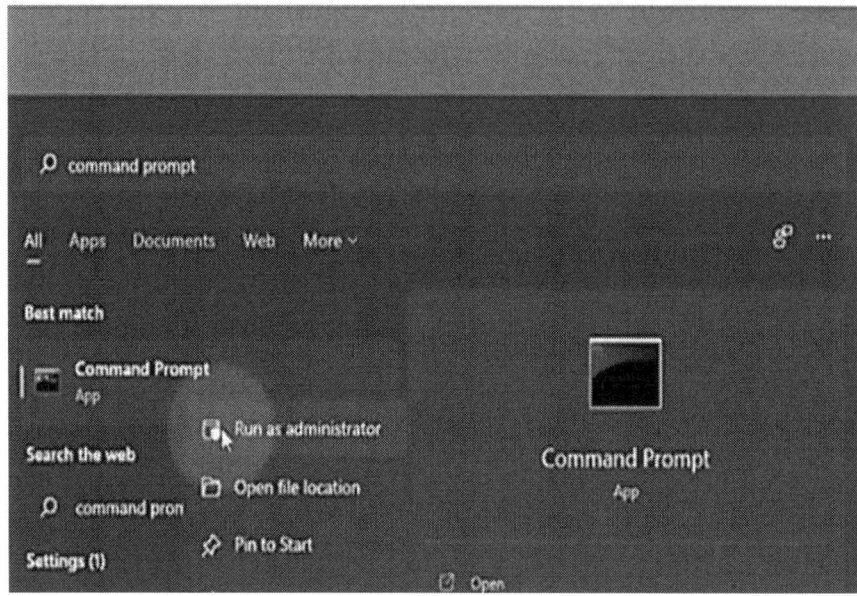

- On the black window, type in **systeminfo** and press Enter

- Below the window, you will see the Hyper-V requirements. If your system is compatible with the requirements, it will be indicated with the word **Yes**.

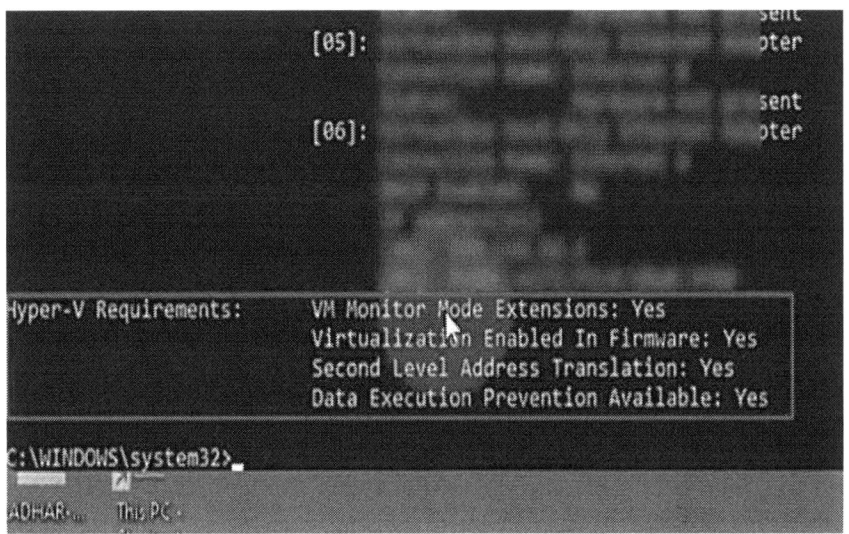

Once your computer is compatible, you can now proceed with the steps below;

- Click on the **Search icon** and search for **Turn Windows features on or off**. Then, click on it.

- Check the **Hyper-V box**, then click **Ok** to begin the installation. To run the Hyper-V, you need to restart your computer.

- After restarting your computer, click on the search icon and search for **Hyper-V Manager**. Then, click on it.

- In the Hyper-V Manager window, on the left-hand side, you will see all the different servers on your system of which one of them will be your computer's name. Click on it. Then on the right-hand side, click on **Quick Create**.

This will open up a prompt where you can specify all the details of your virtual machine. On the left-hand side, select the operating system you want to install. Let's go with the **Ubuntu operating system**. You will have to download the file before you can install it on your virtual machine. If you want to install from an ISO file or a virtual hard disk file, click on the Local installation source option. Once you are done downloading you can now proceed.

- After selecting Ubuntu, on the right-hand side of the prompt, you will see the **(more options)** option, on it, you can give your virtual machine a name, choose your network switch.

- Click on **Create Virtual Machine**. This will kick off the set-up process and your virtual machine will be created.

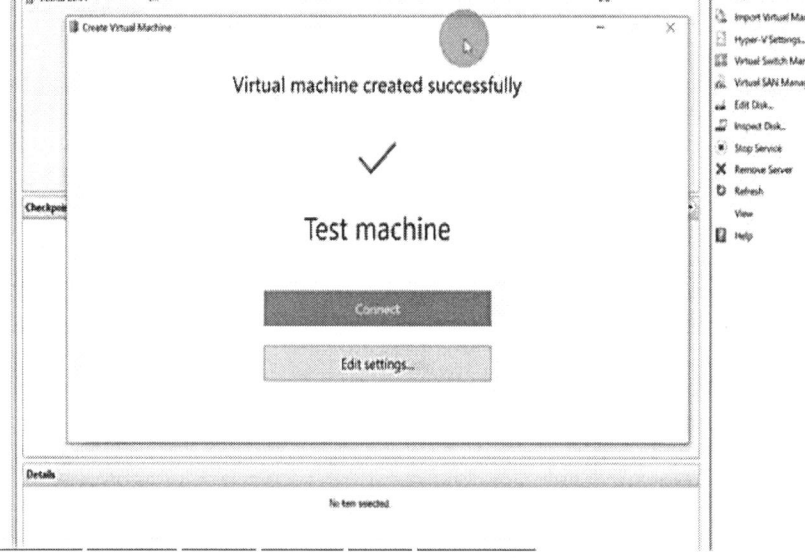

You can connect to it immediately if you want to. You can also choose to edit the settings of the virtual machine.

132

How to install windows 11 to a virtual machine

You may want to install Windows 11 on your computer without it replacing your current Windows. You can do this with the help of a virtual machine. To install Windows 11 on a virtual machine, your PC has to meet up the following requirements;

- Windows 10
- 8GB + Ram
- A 64-Bit Quad Core Processor @2GHz with virtualization support
- At least 50GB of free space on your system

Once it is compatible, follow the steps below to install Windows 11 on a virtual machine;

- Download the **Windows 11 ISO file**. You can download the file from the Microsoft website *www.microsoft.com*

- Download and install the **VMWare workstation player**. VMWare is an application software that emulates the Hardware environments of your operating system and allows you to run more than one operating system on your computer.

- Open the application. Then, create a new virtual machine.

- On the prompt, choose to enable the operating system later and click on **Next.** On the next menu, choose **Microsoft Windows** as the guest operating system and the version as **Windows 10.** Then, click **Next**.

- Create a name for the virtual machine and choose the location where the Windows 11 file will be stored. Allocate the disk space for this virtual machine of at least 60GB. Make sure the host operating system is left with some space. This is to avoid the virtual machine from crashing while running.

- Now, choose to **store the virtual disk as a single file** and click on **Next**.

- Click on **Customize Hardware**. On it, you will allocate to the virtual machine the amount of RAM you want to. You will also choose the processor. Then, Click on **Finish**. Now we are done creating a virtual machine.

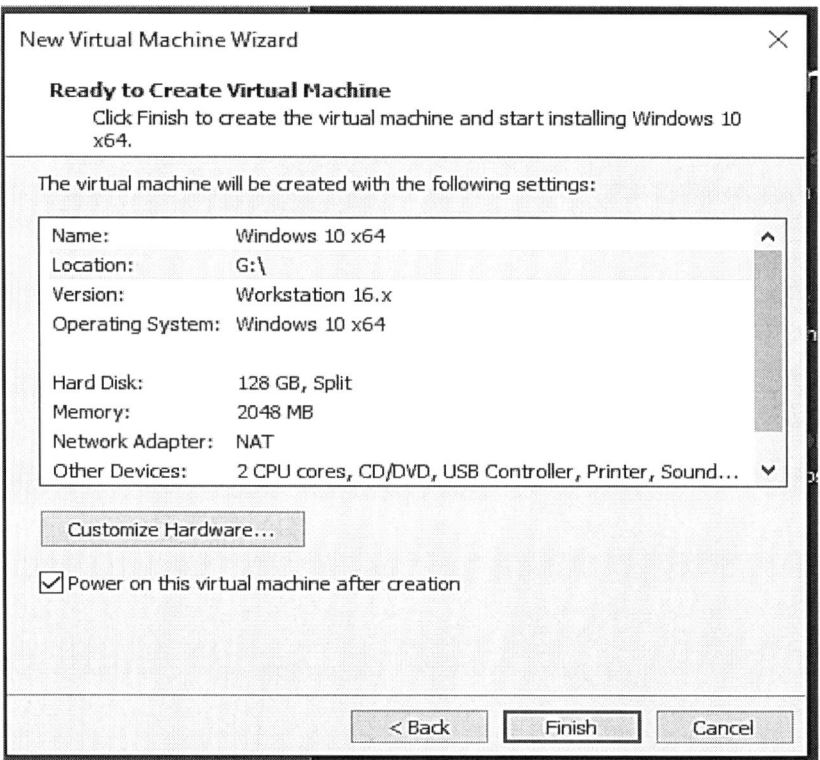

- On the menu of the virtual machine, click on **VM** at the top of the screen, then select **Settings**.

- Go to **CD DVD**. On the Use an ISO file option, click on **Browse**. Locate the Windows 11 ISO file, click on it and select **Open**.

- Once you have done this, you can now start your virtual machine. Press **Enter** on the keyboard, this will boot up the Windows 11 ISO here. You will have to go through the installation process of Windows 11 and once you are done, That's it. You have installed Windows 11 on a virtual machine.

How to install windows 11 on Raspberry pi 4

There are requirements you need to be able to install windows 11 on a Raspberry Pi 4. Below are the requirements;

- Raspberry Pi 4 4GB or 8GB.
- A micro-SD card that has the latest Raspberry Pi OS.
- Windows 10 PC.
- HDMI, Mouse, Keyboard for your Raspberry Pi.
- Bluetooth dongle, Wi-Fi dongle.
- A 32GB or larger SSD via a USB 3 caddy.
- USB boot enabled.
- Internet connection be it Wi-Fi or Ethernet.

To install Windows 11 on a Raspberry Pi OS, follow the instructions below;

- Boot **Raspberry Pi OS**.

- Open a terminal. Then, download and install the **WOR Flasher**. http://github.com/Botspot/wor-flasher

- Put in the **SSD** that the Windows 11 installation will be stored into. Then, **Run** the WOR flasher

- Once it is up and running, you will get a pop-up window. On the pop-up window, select **Windows 11** then choose the model of Raspberry Pi. Click **Next.**

- Choose your language. Click **Next**

- The next window will show you your drive list. Here select the SSD you have plugged in. click on **Refresh** if you don't see it. Then, click Next.

- Your installation overview will be displayed. Click on **Flash**.

This does take about an hour and a half to flash because it needs to download all the files and extract them on the Raspberry Pi using the Quad-core CPU that we have in the Raspberry Pi 4.

- Once it's finished up, it will automatically close the terminal down and give you a window that looks like the image below. The window shows you the extra steps to take to get this started on your Raspberry Pi 4. Click on **Close**.

Next steps:

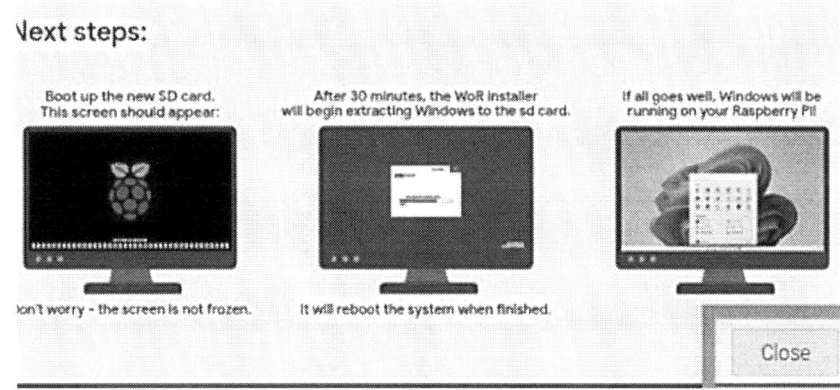

- Now, plug the SSD in the USB port on the Raspberry Pi. Remove the micro-SD card you had Raspberry Pi OS running on. Then, plug the power in.

- When the Raspberry Pi is booting up for the first time, use the **ESC key** on your keyboard to get into the boot setting by pressing it repeatedly. It will be booting from the SSD. Use the arrow keys to navigate.

- On the boot setting menu, select **Raspberry Pi configuration>select Change Display configuration**. **Check** the **720p** option and **uncheck** native resolution. Press the **ESC key** to go back. Press **Y** to save the changes. Then press **Enter**. It will start booting Windows 11. This will take a lot of time.

- After the booting, you can now go through the Windows 11 set-up process.

CHAPTER 28
WINDOWS 11 PRODUCT KEY

Meaning of a product key

A product key on Windows is a code that is used to activate a Windows operating system. It is a 25-character code. When you purchase a physical copy of Windows, the product key is usually found on the label or the card inside the box where the Windows was in. You can also purchase the product key from the Microsoft store. The product key is usually needed when you are reinstalling Windows.

Finding a windows 11 product key

- Click on the **Windows Start** menu and select **Settings**.
- Click on **Update & Security**.
- On the left-hand side of the menu, click on **Activation**.
- The Activation menu will display if your Windows is activated or not. If it is activated, it will display that your **Windows is activated using your organization's activation service**. If it is not activated, you will need to enter a valid Windows key or a digital license gotten from the Microsoft Store.
- Now that your Windows 11 is activated, to find the product key, we will need to make a registry script using a **notepad**.

To make a registry script, simply follow the instructions below;

- Click on the **Search icon** on your taskbar, search for **Notepad**. Then, open it
- On the Notepad menu, type in the following;

Function ConvertToKey(Key)
Const KeyOffset = 52
i = 28
Chars = "BCDFGHJKMPQRTVWXY2346789"
Do
Cur = 0
x = 14
Do
Cur = Cur * 256
Cur = Key(x + KeyOffset) + Cur
Key(x + KeyOffset) = (Cur \ 24) And 255
Cur = Cur Mod 24
x = x -1
Loop While x >= 0
i = i -1
KeyOutput = Mid(Chars, Cur + 1, 1) & KeyOutput
If (((29 – i) Mod 6) = 0) And (i <> -1) Then
i = i -1
KeyOutput = "-" & KeyOutput
End If
Loop While i >= 0
ConvertToKey = KeyOutput
End Function

- Once you are done, click on **File** and select **Save as**.
- Save the file name as a. **VBS File**. For example, **Product key.vbs**
- Save the file type as **All Files**. Then, click **Save**.
- Now, click on the file which will open a window with your Windows 11 Product Key written on it.

How to locate a product key using the command prompt

Using the command prompt to locate your product key is very easy and simple. It is not stressful at all. Okay, you want to find out, Follow the instruction below;

- Click on the **Search icon**. Then, search for **Command Prompt**.
- On the black window, type in the following command and press the **Enter** key.

  'wmic path SoftwareLicensingService get OA3xOriginalProductKey'
- This will display your Windows 11 product key.

Very easy right? It is advisable to keep note of your product key, maybe in a drive or a book to keep it safe in case a new installation of Windows 11 is needed.

BIOS

BIOS stands for Basic Input Output System. It is a very small piece of code contained on a chip on your computer board. When you start your computer, BIOS is the first software that runs. It identifies your computer's hardware, configures it, tests it, and connects it to the operating system for further instructions. This is known as the **boot process**. Entering the BIOS setup utility allows you to change the boot process order as well as a wide variety of hardware settings. It is not recommended for an inexperienced user to change settings in the BIOS unless you are being directed by an experienced person or source.

How to enter bios in windows 11

The standard method for entering the BIOS is to tap a specific function key while the computer is booting. The Function key depends on the model of your computer. The most used function keys are the **Esc key, Delete, F1, F2, F10, F11, or F12**. Some computers also require holding down the **Fn** key while tapping the **F1** or **F2** key.

What is the best way to get into bios from windows?

There are currently two methods for getting into your system's BIOS menu. Both methods are simple and do not necessitate any additional or extra steps to complete. The two methods are using The Function Keys and using The Settings App.

Using the Function Keys

Using the Function keys is the first way to get into your system's BIOS menu. To be able to do this now. Your system must be turned off completely. If it's still running, a simple restart should suffice. You must now press the **F2, F4,** or **F8** key while the system is turned on to access the BIOS menu. To get into the BIOS, you'll have to keep pressing the button. It's worth noting that different OEMs use different buttons to access the BIOS menu. You will be taken to the BIOS menu if you press the right key.

Using the Windows Settings App

You can also use the settings app to access the BIOS menu on your Windows 11 computer. Not everyone can use the Function Key and time it perfectly to enter the BIOS menu every time. Sometimes, the computer will boot too quickly. Follow the instruction below to do so;

- Turn on your Windows 11 PC and go to the **Start Menu**, where you'll find the Settings app icon. Click on it.
- Choose the **Windows Update** option from the Settings app.
- On the Windows Update screen, go to **Advanced Options**.
- In the Advanced Options screen, scroll down a little. Note: The **Recovery option** will appear. Choose it.

- Select **Advanced Startup** from the drop-down menu. Select the **Restart Now** option.

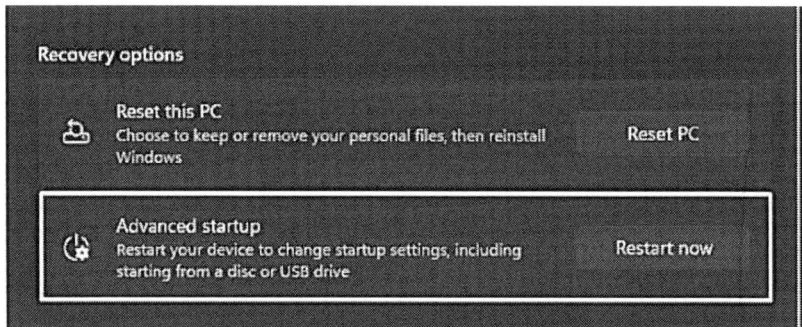

- Before you proceed, double-check that all of your data has been saved.
- The system will restart and you will be sent to the Troubleshooting menu.
- Choose **Troubleshoot** from the drop-down menu.

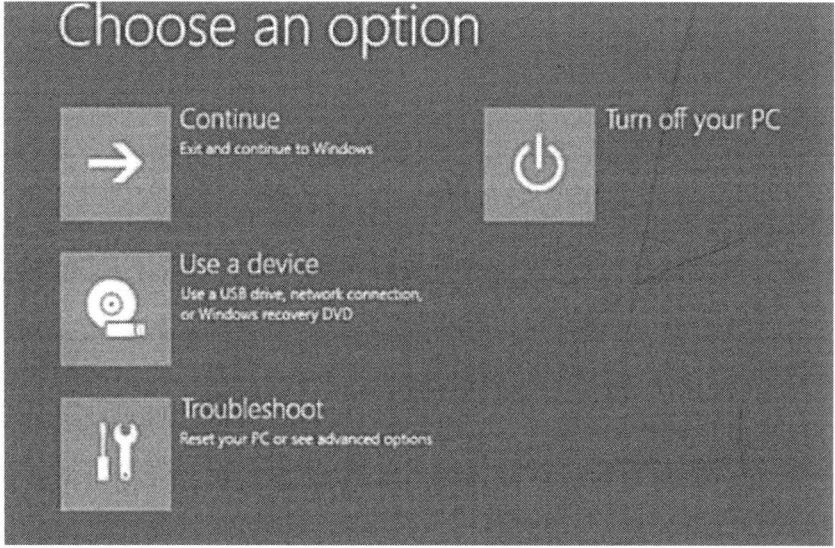

- You'll be given several choices for restarting your computer.

- Choose **UEFI Firmware Settings** from the drop-down menu and select **Restart.**

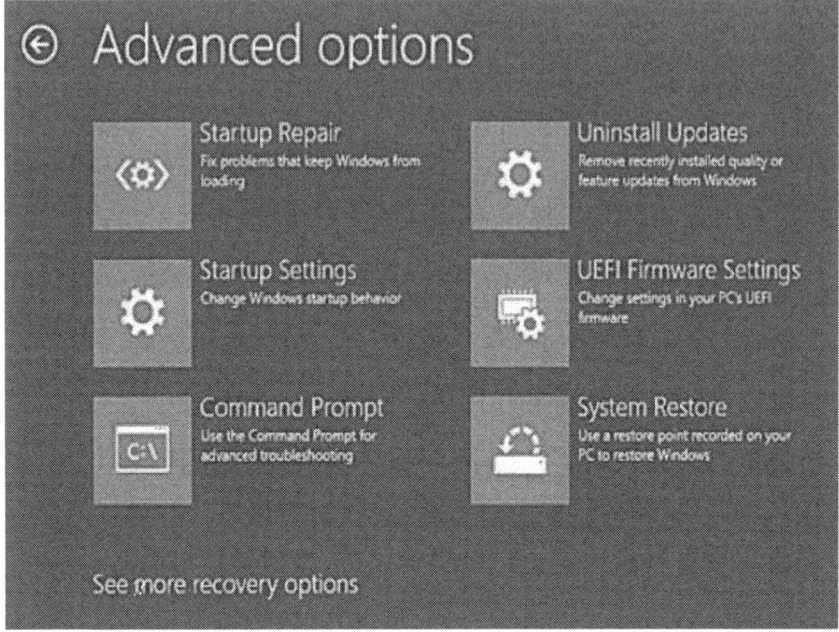

- Your system will now restart and immediately display the BIOS menu.

Advanced Startup

Windows 11's advanced startup settings provide you access to a variety of boot and system recovery options. You may use their assistance to restore Windows 11 to a prior date, restore Windows 11 using a system image, solve boot issues, launch a command prompt window to do various tasks, modify UEFI settings, and restore Windows 11 to a previous build.

In the Windows 11 operating system, there are various methods to obtain extra starting choices.

You can use the Windows Settings or the Power menu to access Advanced Startup settings.

Using the Settings simply,

- Open the Settings app. You may accomplish this by using the **Windows key + I** keyboard shortcut or selecting the gear icon on the Start menu.
- On the right panel of Settings, navigate to the **Recovery settings** group.
- Go to the **Advanced Startup** Options area on the right side and select the **Restart Now** option. You will be able to restart your device right away as a result of this and can access the Advanced Startup menu.
- The "**Select Action**" screen will appear when the machine resumes.
- Click the **troubleshoot** button on the Select Action box.
- Select the **Advanced Settings** tile in the diagnostics box that appears.

Using the Power menu simply,

- Click on the **Windows Start** menu
- Click on the **Power button**.
- Press and hold the **Shift key** then, click the **Restart** button.

This allows you to access the Advanced Startup menu.

IP Address

Your computer will be given a unique IP address regardless of whether you're connected to a Wi-Fi network or a wired connection. Also, you can know your computer's IP address for a variety of reasons. For example, if you wish to connect remotely to your computer or enable access to your device via a firewall, you'll need to get the machine's IP address to log in or authorize the connection to it. There are many methods to get such information in Windows 11. Advanced users can obtain it with a simple command, but not everyone is a power user or advanced.

How to find your IP address on Windows 11

You can find your IP address on Windows 11 in different ways. You can find it with the use of Settings, the Taskbar, and Command Prompt. Let's give you the steps to find it.

Using the taskbar

- Right-click on the **Network icon** on the right-hand side of your taskbar and select Open **Network and Internet settings.**
- Click on **Network and Sharing Center**.
- Click on **Change adapter settings** and right-click on the next option and select **Status.**
- Then, click **Details**. On the details' menu, you will find your IP address alongside other information.

In using the settings, after you have opened it, click on Network & Internet. Then, follow steps 2 and 3 above.

Using Command Prompt

- Click on the **Search icon** and search for **Command Prompt**.
- On the black window, type in **ipconfig** and hit Enter.
- This will display your IP address alongside other information.

CHAPTER 29

BLUETOOTH

Technically, Bluetooth is a universal wireless standard for connecting various digital devices. It is simply a way to eliminate all wires and cables that normally connect devices. Look at some of the desktops we use, where you have to make use of cables to connect the computer to the keyboard, mouse, and monitor. You make use of cables to connect your devices to the computer. Bluetooth has made all these connections easy. With it, you can connect your computer to the keyboard, mouse, and monitor without using wires or cables. We now have Bluetooth computers, mouse, keyboards, phones, tablets, etc. Bluetooth works by transmitting data through radio frequencies and each device is embedded with a transceiver microchip that allows it to connect and communicate with other Bluetooth-enabled devices that are within the range which is about 30 feet or so for most devices.

How to enable Bluetooth on windows 11

Turning on the Bluetooth of your computer can be done in different ways. You can use the Action center to do so. You can also use Windows Settings. We will give you the steps to enable the Bluetooth of your system.

To enable your Bluetooth using the action center, follow the steps outlined below;

- Click on the **Action center** at the right-hand side of your taskbar. You can also use the **Windows key + A** shortcut key to open the Action Center.
- Click on the **Bluetooth icon.**
- That's it, Bluetooth is now enabled. You will see **Not connected** if your device is not paired to any Bluetooth device.

To enable your Bluetooth using settings simply,

- Click on the **Windows Start menu** and select **Settings**.
- Click on **Devices.**
- Turn **ON** the toggle on the Bluetooth option. That's it, the Bluetooth is now enabled.

How to repair Bluetooth using the windows troubleshooter

Have you been trying to connect your Bluetooth with other devices but it does not connect? You can solve that problem using Windows Troubleshooter. Troubleshooting in Windows helps to solve major problems or difficulties in a computer system. Follow the outlined procedures to repair your Bluetooth using Windows troubleshooter;

- Click on the **Windows Start menu** and select **Settings**.
- Select **System.** Scroll down and select **Troubleshoot.**

- On the troubleshooting window, click on **other troubleshooters**.
- Go to the Bluetooth option and click on **Run**.
- This will begin the checking of problems and checking of Bluetooth capability. It will take some time to finish. Once the troubleshooting is complete, try to connect your Bluetooth device.

How to repair Bluetooth using the device manager

Using the device manager to repair your Bluetooth is done in two ways. Using the Update Driver option and the Uninstall option. If you don't have updated driver software, you can update your driver to help repair your Bluetooth.

To repair your Bluetooth using the Update Driver option, simply

- Click on the **Search icon** and search for **Device Manager.**
- Select **Bluetooth.** Then, right-click on the Bluetooth adapter listed below it, and select **Update Driver**, and **Search automatically for updated driver software**. Download and install the driver.
- Once the installation is done, **Restart** your computer and check if the issues have been fixed.

To repair the Bluetooth using the Uninstall Option, simply

- Click on the **Search icon** and search for **Device Manager.**

- Select **Bluetooth**. Right-click on the Bluetooth adapter name, select **Uninstall device** > **Uninstall.**
- **Shut down** your PC. Wait for some seconds after the shutdown before you turn on the PC. The Windows operating system will try to reinstall the driver for your Bluetooth adapter.
- If it doesn't install the driver, go to your **Device Manager**, click on **Action,** then select **Scan for hardware changes.**

Note that you may have to communicate with your PC or other hardware manufacturers to get the latest drivers for your Bluetooth adapter.

How to screenshot on windows 11

Taking screenshots on Windows 11 can be done in different ways. You can choose to screenshot the whole screen; you can as well choose the part of the screen you want to screenshot. Let's give you the ways you can take screenshots on your Windows 11.

1. **Prt Sc Key**: This is one of the simplest ways to screenshot on Windows 11. When you press the PrtSc key, it takes a screenshot of your entire screen. The picture will be copied to your clipboard. If you want to save the image as a file, you will have to paste it into an image editor like Microsoft Paint or Photoshop.

2. **Windows key + Prt Sc key:** When you press the Windows key and the prt sc key, your screen will

become a little bit dark for a second, this means that a screenshot of your screen has been taken. This particular way of taking screenshots on your Windows 11 saves the picture in your computer as a file, you can find it on your File Explorer>Pictures>Screenshots.

3. **Alt key + Prt Sc key:** When you press the keys, it takes a screenshot but it will be copied to your clipboard. This captures only the active window on your screen. For example, if you are on a particular window and a pop-up menu appears on the window you are working on, when you take the screenshot, it captures only the pop-up menu.

4. **Snipping Tool:** You may not want to screenshot your whole screen, you just need to screenshot some sections, this tool helps you to choose the part of the screen you want to screenshot. To open the Snip & Sketch Tool simply press the **Windows Key + Shift Key + S.** This makes your screen turn white but transparent. You can now choose the section of the screen you want to screenshot. Your picture will be copied to your clipboard.

CHAPTER 30
CORTANA

You must have probably heard about Cortana and you are wondering what it is. Cortana is the personal digital assistant built by Microsoft to help assist you in your computer like managing tasks, helping you find out things. It helps you achieve more with less effort. Cortana comes from the Halo games made by Microsoft. Cortana is the name of the artificial intelligence. Cortana on Windows is represented by an icon of circles. Cortana can remind you to do something at a particular time, place, or both. You make use of your voice to give tasks to Cortana. Below is a representation of her in one of the Halo games.

How to enable Cortana on windows 11

Microsoft added Cortana on Windows 10 operating system. It was located on the taskbar. Coming to that of the new operating system Windows 11, it is not located on the taskbar of Windows 11. You might be wondering if it was removed or something. No, Cortana is still available on Windows 11 and we will show you how you can enable it.

To enable Cortana on your Windows 11, follow the instructions below;

- Click on the **Search icon** on your taskbar and search for **Cortana**.

- Click on **Cortana**. Then, click on **Sign-in**. you must have a **Microsoft account** to sign in. If you don't have one, you can create one and sign in.

- Once you are done, click **Continue**.

- The Cortana display menu will appear on the left-hand side of your screen.

- Now, click on the **Windows Start menu** and select **Settings**.

- Click on **Privacy and Security**. On the right-hand side of the menu, under the **App Permission option**, click on **Microphone.**

- Turn **ON** the toggle on the Cortana option.

- Once you have done that, the Cortana menu will appear in the middle of your screen. You have now enabled Cortana and can now communicate with it.

- To disable it, just turn **OFF** the toggle on the Cortana option.

You may want to disable Cortana from starting up when your computer starts up. In doing this you are not entirely disabling it. You can do so by following the steps below;

- Click on the **Windows Start menu** and select **Settings**.

- On the Settings menu, click on **Apps**. Then, select **Apps and Features** on the right-hand side of the menu.

- On the prompt, click on the search bar and type in **Cortana**. Then, click on the **three dots** beside the Cortana option. Then, click on the Advanced **option**.

- Scroll down, under the **Run at log-in** option, turn **OFF** the toggle on the Cortana option.

Command prompt

The Command Prompt has always been a useful tool and is an integral part of Windows. It is used to execute entered commands. You can use it to complete a variety of tasks. With Command Prompt, you can know the list of all installed drivers on your system, your Hardware, and networking information, you can repair and scan your system files, you can check if your server is reachable and so much more.

You may prefer Command Prompt over the traditional GUI (**Graphics User Interface**) approach because it provides a quicker and more comfortable experience and allows you to utilize tools that are not available in the visual interface to resolve problems or complete tasks.

How to open command prompt on windows 11

You can open a Command prompt on your Windows 11; it is quite easy to do this. You can make use of the Windows Terminal, the Search icon on your taskbar, you can also choose to pin a command prompt on your taskbar so that you can easily access it.

How to open command prompt using windows terminal

A terminal program accessible to command-line users is Windows Terminal. PowerShell, Command Prompt, and Azure Cloud Shell are all included. You may start Command Prompt in a new tab or configure the program to open CMD every time it is launched.

To open Command Prompt, simply;

- Right-click the **Windows Start menu** and select **Windows Terminal** from the context menu. Then, select **YES** to continue.

- Click on the dropdown **arrow icon** and select **Command Prompt**. Command Prompt may also be launched by pressing the **CTRL + SHIFT + 2** buttons on the keyboard.

- A new tab will appear with the **CMD** window.

How to set command prompt as a default profile on windows terminal

- Open Windows Terminal settings by clicking the **down arrow symbol** and selecting **Settings.**

- Go to the **Startup** tab, choose **Command Prompt** from the drop-down box under **Default profile**.

- To make the modification permanent, click **Save**. Command Prompt is launched by default when you start Windows Terminal.

To Use the Search icon to launch Command Prompt simply,

- Click the **Search icon** on the taskbar.
- In the search box, type **CMD** or **Command Prompt**, and then click on **Run as administrator** and select **YES.**
- This opens up the Command Prompt menu.

Open Command Prompt from the Taskbar

For people who often use Command Prompt, there is another alternative. By adding it to the Taskbar, you may access it with a single click and save a lot of time. However, Command Prompt must first be pinned to the Taskbar before it can be accessed from there.

- Search for Command Prompt in the 'Search Menu,' right-click on the search result, and choose 'Pin to Taskbar.'
- Simply click on the Command Prompt icon on the Taskbar to launch Command Prompt.

CHAPTER 31

ANDROID APPS ON WINDOWS 11

Applications

An application is a software program that allows you to perform specific tasks. You find applications in most of your devices like your smartphones, computer, and tablets. Some apps help you to complete certain tasks while others are just for fun. Apps that run on your desktop or laptop computers are known as Desktop applications while those apps that run on your smartphones, tablets are known as Mobile Applications. Some of the apps that work on your mobile devices can also work on your computer and vice versa.

Examples of Desktop applications are **Microsoft Office, Web Browsers, Windows Media Player, Games,** etc. Examples of Mobile Applications are **WhatsApp, Instagram, Gmail, Facebook,** etc. Apps are about communication, productivity, entertainment, and more. With so many possibilities you are sure to find several apps that are perfect for the things you do.

How to install android applications on windows 11

Android apps are those applications that run on your smartphone or tablet. The new Windows 11 operating system now allows you to install and run android apps on your system. You will need to install the subsystem for android and also the Amazon store to be able to run them.

To be able to install android apps on your Windows 11, you must first check if your system meets up with the requirements to install them. Below are the requirements you need before you can install android applications;

- The OS build of your system must be **22000** or more.
- The installed RAM should be at least **8 gigabytes**.
- You need to be in the **Beta Channel** of the Windows Insider Program.
- You will enable **virtualization** for your PC. To enable virtualization on your pc, simply click on the **Search icon** on the taskbar and search for **Turn on or off Windows features**. Click on it. On the menu, enable the **Virtual Machine Platform** option and that of the **hypervisor** option.
- You will need to have the latest version of the **Microsoft store**. Go to the settings of the Microsoft store and check for updates. Make sure you have the latest updates.
- The only disappointing thing here is that this only works if your region is set to the **United States**. If you are not in the US region, then you will likely need a **VPN** for it to work. But you can set your region on your system. Simply go to the settings of your computer, search for **region**. Then, on the **country or region** option, make sure that it is set to the United States. This should work but if it doesn't, then you need to use a VPN.
- You need to have a **US-based Amazon account** to use the Amazon Appstore. You can also create that using a VPN.

Once your computer meets up with the requirements, you can now proceed to download and install Windows Subsystem for Android. Simply follow the steps below;

- Open the **Microsoft Store**. On the search box, search for **Amazon Appstore**.
- Click on it and click **Install.** Then, click **Set Up.**
- On the prompt, you will be asked to download the **Windows Subsystem for Android**. Click on **Download.**

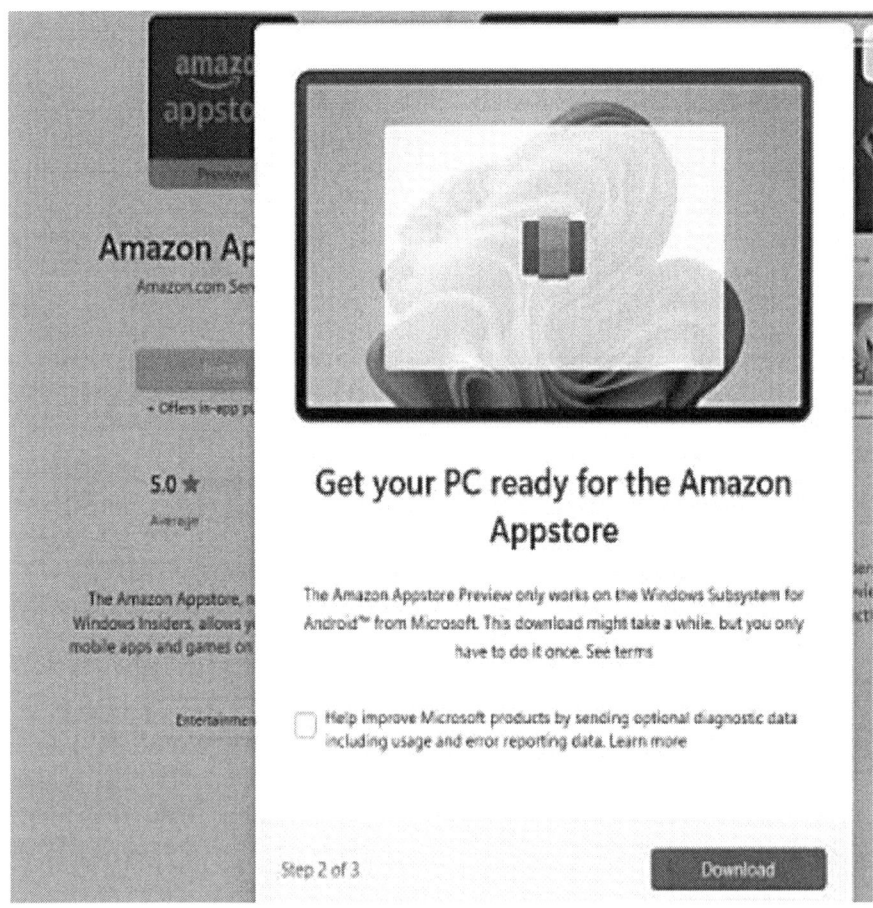

- The download process will take a while. Once the download is done, click **Next**, then **Restart your computer**. After your system has restarted, the Amazon Appstore and the Windows Subsystem for Android should be installed on your PC.

- Now, you will need to set up your Amazon Appstore. You will need to **sign in** with your Amazon account. Once you are done signing in, the Appstore is now ready for you to browse and install Android apps.

To install an Android app, simply,

- Go to the **Amazon Appstore**.
- Search for the App you want to download. Click on the **GET** option to install it on your system.
- The app will be downloaded and will work like other desktop apps on your computer.

You can pin your Android apps to the taskbar or on the Start menu.

CHAPTER 32
CENTRAL PROCESSING UNIT (CPU)

The CPU which stands for Central Processing Unit is the most important part of a computer. It is known as the brain of the computer. It provides processing power to the computer. Everything you do on your computer goes through the CPU which makes it an essential part of every PC. The CPU performs millions of tasks and calculations within a second. All the arithmetic calculations and logical operations take place in the CPU.

The CPU has two parts; The Control Unit and The Arithmetic Logic Unit. The Arithmetic unit is the mathematical brain of the computer. They are responsible for performing addition, subtraction, multiplication, division as well as logical operations on the computer. It does all the computation on the computer. The Control Unit controls all the hardware operations on any computer-like input, output, storage, and processing. It reads and interprets instructions and determines the sequence for processing data.

How to boost your processor or CPU speed on windows 11

The new Windows 11 operating system is known to be very much impressive and faster compared to the other versions. The new features of the operating system, make it offer a unique digital experience. Even with all these features, your processor may be running slow while performing some tasks on your computer. This may be caused by low RAM, too many startup programs running on your operating system, low disk space, malware, and viruses, etc.

So, how can you boost your processor or CPU speed on Windows 11?

There are many ways you can make your windows 11 work faster. We are going to show you the different ways you can do this.

1. **Adjust the Performance Power Plan Settings.**

   - Click on the **Search icon** on your taskbar and search for **Control Panel**. Click on it.

   - Click on the drop-down arrow beside the **view by** option and select **Large files**. Then, click on **Power options**.

   - On the High-performance option, click on **Change plan settings**.

   - Click on **Change advanced power settings**. On the Advanced settings menu, scroll down and select **Processor power management**.

   - On the Minimum processor state, change the settings from **50% to 100**%.

   - On the maximum processor state, change the settings from **50% to 100**%.

   - Then, click **Apply** and **Ok**. Refresh your computer.

2. **Removing the unnecessary/temporary files on your computer.**

- Click on the **Windows Start Button** and select **Settings**.
- Click on **System**, then select **Storage**.
- Click on **Temporary files**.

- Select the files you want to remove, then click on **Remove files**.

3. **Uninstall unnecessary applications**

- Click the **Windows Start button** and select **Settings**.
- Click on **Apps**. On the right-hand side of the menu, click on **Apps and Features**. This will show you a list of the installed apps on your computer.

- Click on the **three dots** beside the apps you want to uninstall, then select **Uninstall**.

4. **Enable the Storage Sense of your computer.**

- Click on the **Windows Start button** and select **Settings**.
- Click on **System**, then select **Storage**.
- On the **Storage Sense** option, turn **ON** the toggle beside it.

When you enable the storage sense of your computer, it automatically helps you free up spaces from your drive and it monitors your computer's storage by removing unnecessary or temporary files and contents.

5. **Disable Startup Apps and programs**

To disable them using settings simply,

- Click on the **Windows Start button** and select **Settings.**
- Click on **Apps**. Then, click on **Startup**.
- Now, turn **OFF** the toggle for the apps you don't want to start automatically.

To disable them using the Task manager simply,

- Click on the **Search icon** and search for **Task Manager**.
- Click on the **Startup** tab.
- Right-click on the program you want to remove from the startup and select **Disable.**

Some Startup apps and programs can configure themselves to start automatically and they keep running in the background. This consumes memory and storage and can slow down the speed of your processor.

How To Backup Your Files on Windows 11

A backup is a copy of a file that is stored separately from the main file which can be used to restore the main file if it is lost or damaged. You may want to format your computer and would not like to lose your files; you can back up your files on your Windows 11 to avoid losing the files. To do so, follow the outlined procedure below;

- Click on the **Search icon** and search for Control Panel. Then, click on it.
- Under the **System and Security**, click on **Backup and Restore**.
- Click on **Set up backup**.
- On the next menu, select where you want to save your backup. You must have an external drive connected to your computer. Then, click on **Next**.
- On the next menu, choose what you want to backup and click on **Next**.
- Click on **Save settings and run backup.**
- Your backup process will start.

How to create a full backup of your computer to an external hard drive on windows 11

A full backup means creating a copy of everything on your computer including the Windows 11 installation files, settings, apps, and your files. You can do this on Windows 11 with the **System image backup feature** which is a feature deprecated on this version but it is still available and you can at least use it to create a temporary backup when you need to replace a hard drive or rollback after an upgrade. If you want to keep an up-to-date backup of your files, you should be using the **File history feature** or a cloud service like **OneDrive** except you are proactive and you create a full backup every day.

Here's how you can create a full backup of Windows 11 to an external hard drive.

- First, connect **the USB drive** (the drive must have enough space to store the files).
- Click on the **Search icon** and search for **Control Panel**. Click on it.
- Click on **System and Security**.
- Click on **File History**.
- Click on the **System Backup Image** option at the bottom left-hand side of the prompt. Then, click on the **Create a System Image** option on the upper left-hand side of the prompt.
- Select the Drive you want to back up your computer and then click **Next**.
- On the next menu, if you have more than one hard drive connected, you can select the other drives. Then, click on the **Start backup** button to create the backup.
- Once the full backup has been completed, you will get this prompt to create a system repair disk. You can choose to ignore this option because you can use the **advanced setup settings** on Windows 11 to access the recovery tools. You can also use the Windows 11 USB bootable media to access the same feature.

To restore your computer using a backup,

- Click on the **Windows Start button** and click on **Settings.**

- Click on **System**. Then, on the right-hand side of the menu, click on **Recovery**.

- On the Advanced setup option, click on the **Restart now**.

- On the advanced setup settings menu, click on **Troubleshoot**.

- Click on **Advanced options**. Then, click on **See more recovery options**.

- Click on **System Image Recovery**. Before you go to this option, make sure to connect the USB drive to the computer.

- **Select Use the latest available system image**. The date of the backup you are restoring will be available. If you have different backups, you can also select the backup from the list by clicking on the **Select a system image** option. Then, click **Next**.

- On the next menu, since you are restoring with the same hard drive click on **Next**. (If you are not using the same hard drive or you are using a brand-new drive to restore the backup, select the **format and repartition the disks option**). Click **Next**.

- Click on the **Finish button**. The backup has been restored.

- Click on **Continue** on the Advanced startup menu and this takes you to your Windows 11 desktop.

How to factory reset on windows 11

Factory reset cleans and reboots the entire system of the computer. It makes the computer function again in a new form. If you don't back up your files before performing the factory reset, you will lose the files. A factory reset clears everything on your computer except the software which will be restored to its default state.

To factory reset on Windows 11, just

- Click on the **Windows Start button** and select **Settings**.
- Click on **Update and Security**. Then, click on **Recovery**.
- On the right-hand side of the Recovery menu, click on **Reset this PC**.
- On the next menu, you will be given two options; if you would want to keep your files or remove everything.
- If you click on the keep your files option, you will be asked how you want to reinstall your Windows operating system. If you want to download it using **Local reinstall** or from **Cloud**.
- If you select the Cloud option, it will download Windows (from Cloud Servers) and install it on your computer and this will take a lot of time depending on your internet connection. If you select the Local

reinstall option, it will reinstall Windows using the already installed Windows. This does not take a lot of time. Most people go with the local reinstall option.

- After you have made your choice, the next menu shows you the outcomes of resetting your computer.
- Once you are done reading the outcomes, click on the **Reset button** to begin the process. This will take some time to finish resetting the Windows and do not interrupt the power connected to the PC. If in the process, you have a power failure, the installation process will corrupt and the current operating system may not be accessible and because of that, you will have to install Windows from the beginning.
- When the resetting is complete, it will direct you to the login interface. When you log in, it begins to customize your Windows settings just like the settings you make when you install Windows for the first time.

CHAPTER 33

WINDOWS 11 SHORTCUTS KEYS

The newly added shortcut keys to Windows 11 have been discussed in this earlier chapter of this guide. Here, we will be looking at the overall shortcut keys attributed to Windows 11; these shortcuts function in Layouts, Widgets, Quick Settings, and Action Center. Let's take a detailed look at them.

Newly Added Shortcuts in Windows 11

As a reminder, below are the newly added shortcut keys

Action	Shortcut
Opening Action Center	**Win + A**
Opening Notifications Panel (Notification Center)	**Win + N**
Opening Widgets Panel	**Win + W**
Quick Access to Snap Layout	**Win + Z**
Open Microsoft Teams	**Win + C**

Text-Editing Shortcuts

Action	Shortcut
Cutting the selected item	**Ctrl + X**
Copying the selected item	**Ctrl + C**
Paste the selected item	**Ctrl + V**
Bolden selected text	**Ctrl + B**
Italicize selected text	**Ctrl + I**
Underline selected text	**Ctrl + U**
Moving the cursor to the start of the current line	**Home**
Moving the cursor to the end of the current line	**End**

General Shortcuts Keys in Windows 11

Action	Shortcut
Switch between open apps.	**Alt + Tab**
Close the active item, or exit the active app.	**Alt + F4**
Lock your PC.	**Win + L**

Display and hide the desktop.	**Win + D**
Perform the command for that letter.	**Alt + underlined letter**
Display properties for the selected item.	**Alt + Enter**
Open the shortcut menu for the active window.	**Alt + Spacebar**
Go back.	**Alt + Left arrow**
Go forward.	**Alt + Right arrow**
Move up one screen.	**Alt + Page Up**
Move down one screen.	**Alt + Page Down**
Close the active document	**Ctrl + F4**
Select all items in a document or window	**Ctrl + A**
Delete the selected item and move it to the Recycle Bin	**Ctrl + D**
Refresh the active window	**Ctrl + R**

Redo an action.	**Ctrl + Y**
Move the cursor to the beginning of the next word.	**Ctrl + Right arrow**
Move the cursor to the beginning of the previous word.	**Ctrl + Left arrow**
Move the cursor to the beginning of the next paragraph	**Ctrl + Down arrow**
Move the cursor to the beginning of the previous paragraph.	**Ctrl + Up arrow**
Use the arrow keys to switch between all open apps	**Ctrl + Alt + Tab**
When a group of tiles is in focus on the Start menu, move it in the direction specified.	**Alt + Shift + arrow keys**
When a tile is in focus on the Start menu, move it into another tile to create a folder.	**Ctrl + Shift + arrow keys**
Resize the Start menu when it's open.	**Ctrl + arrow keys**
Select multiple individual items in a window or on the desktop	**Ctrl + arrow**

	key+ spacebar
Select a block of text	**Ctrl + Shift with an arrow key**
Open Start.	**Ctrl + Esc**
Open Task Manager	**Ctrl + Shift + Esc**
Switch the keyboard layout when multiple keyboard layouts are available	**Ctrl + Shift**
Turn the Chinese input method editor (IME) on or off.	**Ctrl + Spacebar**
Display the shortcut menu for the selected item.	**Shift + F10**
Delete the selected item without moving it to the Recycle Bin first	**Shift + Delete**
Open the next menu to the right, or open a submenu	**Right arrow**
Open the next menu to the left, or close a submenu	**Left arrow**
Stop or leave the current task	**Esc**

Take a screenshot of your whole screen **PrtScn** and copy it to the clipboard.

Function Shortcut Keys

Action	Shortcut
Rename the selected item.	**F2**
Search for a file or folder in File Explorer.	**F3**
Display the address bar list in File Explorer.	**F4**
Refresh the active window.	**F5**
Cycle through screen elements in a window or on the desktop.	**F6**
Activate the Menu bar in the active app	**F10**
Maximize or minimize the active window	**F11**

File Explorer Shortcut Keys

Action	Shortcut
Select the address bar.	**Alt + D**
Select the search box	**Ctrl + E**

Open a new window	**Ctrl + N**
Close the active window	**Ctrl + W**
Change the size and appearance of file and folder icons	**Ctrl + mouse scroll wheel**
Display all folders above the selected folder	**Ctrl + Shift + E**
Create a new folder	**Ctrl + Shift + N**
Display all subfolders under the selected folder	**Num Lock + asterisk (*)**
Display the contents of the selected folder	**Num Lock + plus (+)**
Collapse the selected folder	**Num Lock + minus (-)**
Display the preview panel	**Alt + P**
Open the Properties dialog box for the selected item	**Alt + Enter**
View the next folder	**Alt + Right arrow**
View the folder that the folder was in	**Alt + Up arrow**

View the previous folder	**Alt + Left Arrow or Backspace**
Display the current selection	**Right arrow**
Collapse the current selection	**Left arrow**
Display the bottom of the active window	**End**
Display the top of the active window	**Home**

Taskbar Shortcut Keys

Action	Shortcut
Open an app or quickly open another instance of an app.	**Shift + left click app icon**
Open an app as an administrator	**Ctrl + Shift + left click a app icon**
Show the window menu for the app	**Shift + right-click app icon**
Cycle through apps in the taskbar	**Win + T**
Open apps in the taskbar based on their pinned number	**Win + Number key**

Cycle through the windows of the group	**Ctrl + click a grouped taskbar button**

Settings Shortcut Keys

Action	Shortcut
Open settings	**Win + I**
Go back to the settings home page	**Backspace**
Search settings	**Type on any page with a search box**

Virtual Desktops Shortcut Keys

Action	Shortcut
Open Task view	**Win + Tab**
Add a virtual desktop	**Win + Ctrl + D**
Switch between virtual desktops you've created on the right	**Win + Ctrl + Right arrow**
Switch between virtual desktops you've created on the left	**Win + Ctrl + Left arrow**

Action	Shortcut
Close the virtual desktop you're using	Win + Ctrl + F4

Dialog Box Shortcuts Keys

Action	Shortcut
Display the items in the active list	F4
Move back through tabs	Ctrl + Shift + Tab
Move back through tabs	Ctrl + Shift + Tab
Move to nth tab	Ctrl + number (number 1–9)
Move forward through options	Tab
Perform the command (or select the option) that is used with that letter	Alt + underlined letter
Select or clear the check box if the active option is a check box	Spacebar

Open a folder one level up if a folder is selected in the Save As or Open dialog box	**Backspace**
Select a button if the active option is a group of option buttons	**Arrow keys**

Command Prompt Shortcut Keys

Action	Shortcut
Copy the selected text	**Ctrl + C**
Paste the selected text	**Ctrl + V**
Enter Mark mode.	**Ctrl + M**
Begin selection in block mode	**Alt + selection key**
Move the cursor in the direction specified	**Arrow keys**
Move the cursor by one page up	**Page up**
Move the cursor by one page down	**Page down**
Move the cursor to the beginning of the buffer	**Ctrl + Home**

Move the cursor to the end of the buffer	**Ctrl + End**
Move up one line in the output history	**Ctrl + Up arrow**
Move down one line in the output history	**Ctrl + Down arrow**

Game Bar Shortcut Keys

Action	Shortcut
Open Game Bar	**Win + G**
Take a screenshot of the active game	**Win + Alt + PrtSc**
Record the last 30 seconds of the active game	**Win + Alt + G**
Start or stop recording active game	**Win + Alt + R**
Show/ hide recording timer of active game	**Win + Alt + T**

Accessibility Shortcut Keys

Action	Shortcut
Turn on Magnifier and Zoom	**Win + plus (+)**
Zoom out using Magnifier	**Win + minus (-)**
Open "Ease of Access" Centre in Windows Settings	**Win + U**
Exit Magnifier	**Win + Esc**
Switch to the docked mode in Magnifier	**Alt + Ctrl + D**
Switch to full-screen mode in Magnifier	**Alt + Ctrl + F**
Turn Sticky Keys on or off	**Press Shift five times**
Switch to lens mode in Magnifier	**Alt + Ctrl + L**
Invert colors in Magnifier	**Alt + Ctrl + I**
Cycle through views in Magnifier	**Alt + Ctrl + M**
Resize the lens with the mouse in Magnifier	**Alt + Ctrl + R**
Pan in Magnifier	**Alt + Ctrl + Arrow keys**

Action	Shortcut
Zoom in or out	**Ctrl + Alt + mouse scroll**
Open Narrator	**Win + Enter**
Turn Toggle Keys on or off	**Press Num Lock for five seconds**
Open on-screen keyboard with this shortcut in Windows 11	**Win + Ctrl + O**
Turn Filter Keys on and off	**Hold down Right Shift for eight seconds**
Turn High Contrast on or off	**Left Alt + Left Shift + PrtSc**
Turn Mouse Keys on or off	**Left Alt + Left Shift + Num Lock**

Browser Shortcut Keys

Action	Shortcut
Find on page	Ctrl + F
Select the URL in the address bar to edit	Alt + D
Open "Ease of Access" Centre in Windows Settings	Win + U
Open History	Ctrl + H

Open Downloads in a new tab	**Ctrl + J**
Open a new window	**Ctrl + N**
Print the current page	**Ctrl + P**
Reload the current page	**Ctrl + R**
Open a new tab and switch to it	**Ctrl + T**

Congratulations!

We've come to the end of the training course of Microsoft Windows 11, I believe the whole chapters and each section of the book will serve as a guideline to you. Thank you for taking the time to study this book.

Did you know?

Positive reviews from awesome customers/readers like you help others to feel confident about making their choice. Could you take 60 seconds and share your happy experiences? This helps us to continue providing great products and helps potential buyers to make confident decisions.

Thank you in advance for your review and for being a preferred customer.

Printed in Poland
by Amazon Fulfillment
Poland Sp. z o.o., Wrocław
01 March 2022

9a3871ed-e74c-41ac-b09a-1a96aed97030R01